THE CATHOLIC UNIVERSITY OF AMERICA
CANON LAW STUDIES
No. 137

DIOCESAN ARCHIVES

A HISTORICAL SYNOPSIS AND COMMENTARY

A DISSERTATION

Submitted to the Faculty of Canon Law of the Catholic University of America in Partial Fulfillment of the Requirements for the Degree of
DOCTOR OF CANON LAW

BY

WILLIAM FRANCIS LOUIS, J. C. L.
Priest of the Diocese of Paterson

THE CATHOLIC UNIVERSITY OF AMERICA PRESS
WASHINGTON, D. C.
1941

Nihil obstat:
Eduardus Roelker,
Censor Deputatus.

Imprimatur:
✠ Thomas H. McLaughlin,
Bishop of Paterson.

September 22, 1941.

PRINTED IN THE UNITED STATES OF AMERICA
BY ST. ANTHONY GUILD PRESS, PATERSON, N. J.

TO MY FATHER

and to the memory of

MY MOTHER

FOREWORD

The necessity for archives should be obvious. The practice of keeping them arises out of the very nature of good administration. So limited is the memory of man that the business of a single day will soon be forgotten if it is not put down in writing, and its records preserved. The recognition of this fact by executives and administrators in every field, together with their obligation of safeguarding important documents, impresses upon these officials the need of arranging the writings in an orderly manner and of having them in a place where they are carefully protected. Consequently, in the secular world, almost all nations, industries and organized societies, however small and humble they may be, maintain some form of archives, and often at great expense.

If so much diligence is used with regard to worldly affairs, much more carefully should be preserved the letters, records and documents which belong to the Church and which, in some instances, are the basis for spiritual or temporal rights of her members. Many of these writings, because of their nature and purpose, are kept in the office of a bishop. So intimately interwoven are they with his work that they constitute the source material for almost all matters *in foro externo* of the diocese, and are to be the permanent record of his whole administration. So diocesan archives are a natural outgrowth of the bishop's duties. The importance attached to their careful maintenance and custody is borne out by the Code of Canon Law, in which the legislation on this subject is so detailed as to embrace ten canons.[1]

But despite the necessity and importance of diocesan archives and the stress laid upon them by the present law, little attention seems to have been given to the ecclesiastical laws regarding them by canonical commentators either before or since the Code. Most modern authors merely repeat the Church's enactments on the subject with little or no explanation. Therefore it is hoped that the present study may stimulate greater interest in the legislation pertaining to this function of the bishop's office.

The aim of this dissertation is to trace the legal history of diocesan archives and to present a commentary on the pertinent canons of the

1. Cc. 375-384.

Code. A consideration of other ecclesiastical archives, such as those of the Vatican, of parishes, of monasteries and the like, and a study of the value and authority of the documents contained in diocesan archives, are topics beyond the scope of this work, and any reference to them has been made only by way of illustration to assist in the examination of the subject at hand. A brief treatment of certain general notions such as the definition of the word *archives,* the employment of various terms for this word in history, the purpose and use of early secular archives and of ecclesiastical archives in general, constitutes an aid by way of introduction to the historical study of diocesan archives and has consequently been offered in a preliminary chapter.

The historical development is considered in two chapters. Since there was little legislation enacted during the first sixteen centuries, the first of these chapters is rather brief. It merely establishes the fact that diocesan archives were of early origin and were in use quite universally throughout this long period. The second chapter considers the conciliar legislation and the principal legislative documents concerning diocesan archives which appeared during the four centuries anterior to the Code.

The principal documents are the constitutions *"Muneris nostri"* of Pope St. Pius V, March 1, 1571; *"Provida"* of Pope Sixtus V, April 29, 1587; and *"Maxima vigilantia"* of Pope Benedict XIII, June 14, 1727. While these constitutions contained only particular legislation, they directly influenced local conciliar enactments in many places, and are the real sources for the canons in the Code. Especially is this true of the constitution *"Maxima vigilantia"* of Pope Benedict XIII.

In the consideration of this earlier legislation regarding diocesan archives, the method used selects the salient features of the pontifical documents and of the particular conciliar legislation. These features relate to the *erection, contents, custody* and *use* of diocesan archives and the *penalties* decreed for violations of the laws enacted. Under these headings each topic has been considered at length in its whole development. This method seemed preferable to the exclusive study of the details of each pontifical constitution, for the present law unfolds itself in this same manner, treating the topics in a similar order.

The canons in the Code deal with general or common diocesan

archives and with secret diocesan archives. Accordingly the canonical commentary has been divided into two chapters. Throughout the commentary an effort has been made to anticipate questions that may arise concerning the meaning of the laws regulating both archives, and to answer them, as far as possible, in a practical manner. In the first chapter of the commentary, however, an article concerning the arrangement of diocesan archives includes a suggested method of filing, to formulate which information was gathered by means of visits to various diocesan chanceries and through numerous inquiries made of priests familiar with the subject. Although not strictly canonical, the article seems most apposite to a work of this kind.

The writer wishes at this time to acknowledge his obligation of gratitude to His Excellency, the Most Reverend Thomas H. McLaughlin, S. T. D., Bishop of Paterson, whose kindly interest and generosity have enabled the author to pursue graduate studies at the Catholic University of America. This occasion is also gladly taken to express the writer's deep appreciation of the direction and assistance he received from the members of the Faculty of the School of Canon Law. Among others also the author is indebted to the Rev. Anthony A. Esswein, J. C. D., and the Rev. Cyril Shircel, O. F. M., who graciously assisted in the preparation of this work

TABLE OF CONTENTS

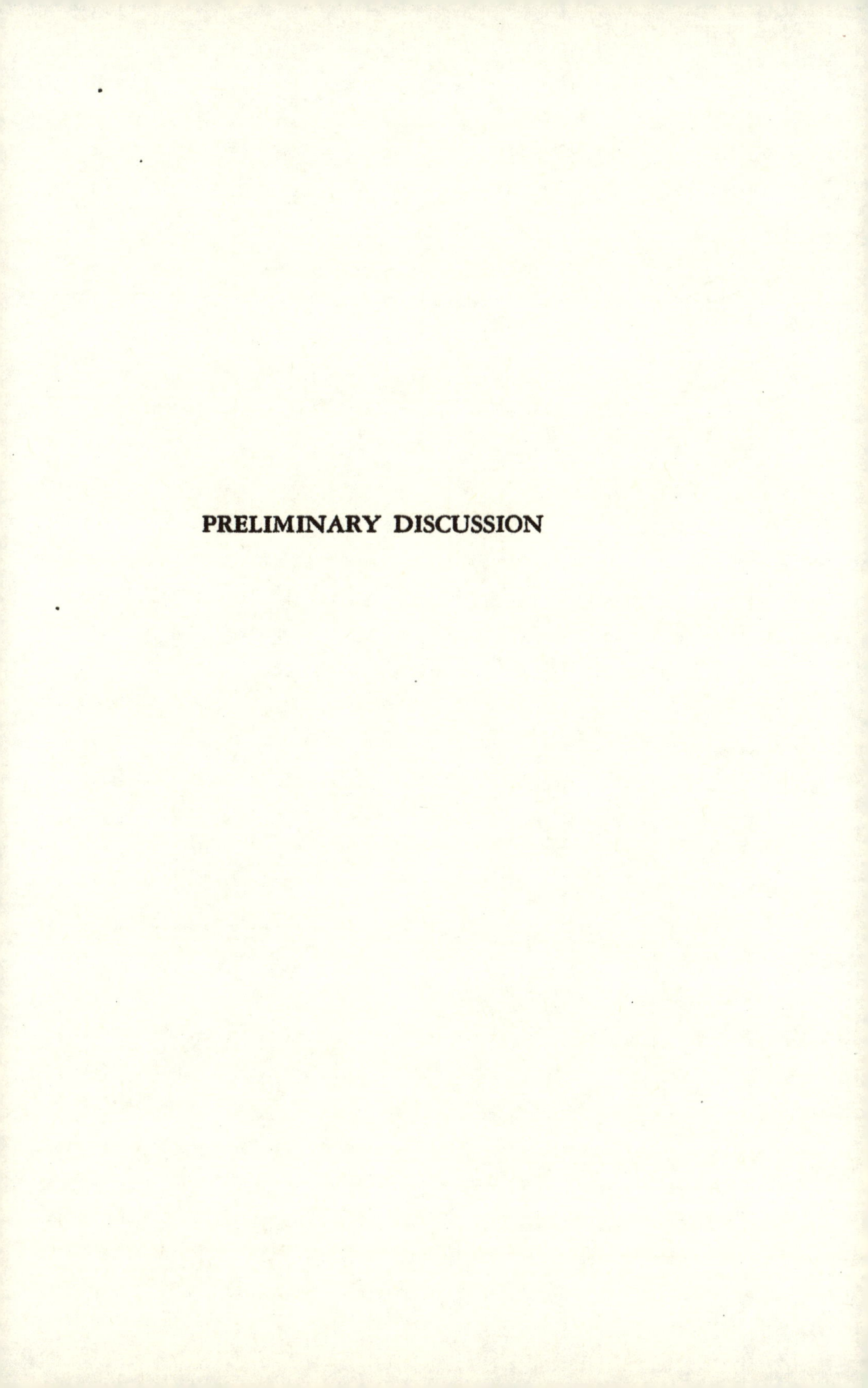

PRELIMINARY DISCUSSION

CHAPTER I

PRELIMINARY NOTIONS

Article 1. Definition and Various Terms Used for the Word *Archives*

The word *archives* is derived from the Greek word αρχεῖον, meaning the senate-house, town hall or the office or residence of the chief magistrate; and from the plural form αρχεῖα, meaning public documents. For this reason, in the course of time, the term has acquired a twofold significance, denoting either a place in which documents or papers are stored, or the documents or papers themselves, in the original or in copies. Since it is the sense most frequently employed the first meaning will be adopted in the present work, and *archives* will be understood as *a place where documents and writings are deposited in order to insure their preservation.*

The meaning associated with the word *archives* has been given expression by many different terms in the past. In the works of Cicero[1] and of Vergil[2] this meaning was expressed by the term *tabularium,* which word is still retained by the Code.[3] Pliny called archives *tablina*[4] and *scrinium,*[5] the latter term being one of the expressions most commonly used throughout history. The Latin derivatives of the original Greek word are many and varied. *Archivum* is used very frequently, but such forms as *arca* and *arcivum*[6] or *archivus*[7] are found.

1. *Pro Archia,* 4. 8 — Clark, *M. Tullii Ciceronis Orationes* (Oxonii, 1910), 4. 7.

2. *Georgicon, II,* 502 — Benoist, *Oeuvres de Virgile,* Texte Latin (Paris, 1876), p. 194.

3. C. 375, § 1, *archivum seu tabularium.*

4. *Nat. Hist.,* XXXV, 2. 2. (7) — *C. Plinii Secundi, Naturalis Historiae Libri XXXVII,* ex Editione Gabriel Brotier (Londini, 1826), X, 4540.

5. *Nat. Hist.,* VII, 26 — *Ibidem,* III, 1340.

6. St. Isidore, *Etymologiarum,* Lib. XX — Migne, *Patrologiae Cursus Completus, Series Latina* (Paris, 1844-1864), LXXXII, 719. (Hereafter this work will be cited as *MPL*).

7. Council of Mileve (402), c. LXXXVI — Mansi, *Sacrorum Conciliorum Nova et Amplissima Collectio,* III, 786. (Hereafter this collection will be referred to as Mansi).

Just as in the English language today, so also the use of the plural *archiva* appeared more often in the Latin than the singular form. Very common, too, was the word *chartophylacium,* especially when it was employed to refer to archives in Constantinople.[8] Other words, such as *grammaphylacium,* used by Ulpian,[9] *chartarium*[10] and *chartarum tomi*[11] are mentioned but rarely. More recently the words *conditoria* and *armaria* are also found in an important papal document on this subject.[12]

Article 2. Early Secular Archives

The necessity of archives was recognized very early in history and we find them in use among the most ancient peoples. In the First Book of Esdras reference is made to archives in which were kept the acts of the kings of Babylon.[13] Tertullian speaks of the archives of the ancient Egyptians, Chaldeans and Phoenicians.[14] With the early Greeks the temples of each city and town were the locations of archives, where not only the documents of general interest to the citizens were preserved, but also the originals of poems honoring the country.[15] That there were archives in use during the early periods of Roman civilization is clear from the words of Cicero, who speaks of archives having been burned during the Italian Civil War;[16] of

8. III Council of Constantinople (680), Actio XII — Mansi, XI, 558; St. Gregory the Great (590-604), *Registri epistolarum libri XIV,* Lib. IX, Ep. 122 — *MPL,* LXXVII, 1056, *et al.*

9. D. (48.19) 9.6.

10. St. Jerome, *Apologia adversus libros Rufini,* Lib. 3, n. 20 — *MPL,* XXIII, 471.

11. St. Gregory of Tours, *Historicae ecclesiasticae Francorum libri X,* Lib. X, c. 19 — *MPL,* LXXI, 552.

12. Benedict XIII, constitution "*Maxima vigilantia,*" June 14, 1727 — *Bullarium Diplomatum et Privilegiorum Sanctorum Romanorum Pontificum, Tauriensis Editio* (25 vols. Augustae Taurinorum, 1857-1872), XXII, 560. (Hereafter this collection will be referred to as *Bullarium Romanum*).

13. I Esdras, VI, 1-12.

14. *Apologia,* Cap. 19 — *MPL,* I, 387.

15. *Encyclopédie des Gens du Monde* (22 vols., Paris, 1833-1844), II, 199.

16. *Pro Archia,* 4. 8 — Clark, *M. Tullii Ciceronis Orationes,* 4. 7.

Vergil, who mentions "archives of the people",[17] and of Pliny, who tells of the archives of Pompeius and Scipio being seized and burned,[18] and of archives being filled with codices and documents.[19] Tertullian writes that in his time the Roman archives still contained the census of Caesar Augustus which recorded the Nativity of Our Lord.[20]

A decree of the Emperor Justinian (527-565) provided that throughout all the provinces of his empire there were to be erected in every city public buildings wherein the records of the civil officials were to be kept, and that in each province some person was to be appointed to have custody over them.[21] Pope St. Gregory the Great (590-604) mentions, however, that Justinian's own archives had already been burned by the time of his Pontificate, and that hardly any documents had been saved.[22] Archives were also used among the nations that sprang up later outside the Roman Empire. Under the Emperor Charlemagne (800-814) an important office was that of the chancellor, who had care of the royal archives,[23] and Keneth, King of the Scots (840-855) placed *jurisperiti* in charge of the archives of that country.[24]

Article 3. Ecclesiastical Archives in General

Just as the civil governments, so also the Church kept archives from the earliest times. Indications of this can be seen in the action of Pope St. Clement I (90-99) who appointed notaries to record the

17. *Georgicon, II,* 502 — Benoist, *Oeuvres de Virgile,* Texte Latin, p. 194.

18. *Nat. Hist.,* VII, 26 — *C. Plinii Secundi, Naturalis Historiae Libri XXXVII,* III, 1340.

19. *Nat. Hist.,* XXXV, 2. 2 (7). — *Ibidem,* X, 4540.

20. *Adv. Marcion 4,* Cap. 7 — *MPL,* II, 370.

21. N. (15.5) 2.

22. *Registri epistolarum libri XIV,* Lib. IX,. Epis. 122 — *MPL,* LXXVII, 1056.

23. Thomassinus, *Vetus et Nova Ecclesiae Disciplina, De Beneficiis,* Pars I, Lib. II, cap. 105, n. 1. (Hereafter this work will be referred to simply as *Thomassinus*).

24. *Ecclesiastical Laws of Keneth, King of Scots,* n. III — Harduin, *Acta Conciliorum et Epistolae Decretales ac Constitutiones Summorum Pontificum* (12 vols., Parisiis, 1715), IV, 1454. (Hereafter this collection will be cited as Harduin).

Acts of the Martyrs.[25] Similar records were diligently compiled also by Pope St. Anterus (235).[26] St. Augustine mentions ecclesiastical archives in one of his epistles,[27] and by the sixth century they were held in great honor.[28] When the public archives of kings were destroyed by the ravages of time or by fire, Divine Providence often preserved the archives of the monasteries and of the churches.[29]

Ecclesiastical archives have always had as their model those of the Holy See, the Mother Church and the head of the others. In the middle of the fourth century, under Pope St. Sylvester (314-335), they were already famous.[30] St. Jerome recommended the consulting of them,[31] and during the subsequent centuries they were constantly referred to in connection with the affairs of the Church in every part of the world.[32] These papal archives were first established by Pope St. Damasus (366-394) near the Basilica of S. Lorenzo in Damaso, but by the year 649 they had been moved to the Lateran. During the reign of Pope Innocent III (1198-1216) they were erected near St. Peter's in the Vatican. For various reasons the archives were moved in the fourteenth century to Agnani, Perugia, Lucca, Assisi and finally to Avignon, from which transfers the valuable contents suffered great losses. They were partly returned to Rome in 1441, but not completely restored until 1784. Under Pope Paul V the

25. Baronius, *Annales Ecclesiastici,* II (Barri-Ducis, 1864), 601.

26. *Loc. cit.*

27. *Epis. 43, Ad Gloriam — MPL,* XXXIII, 172.

28. *Dictionnaire Raisonné de Diplomatique Chrétienne* (Paris, 1846), s. v. "Archives Ecclésiastiques," col. 89.

29. Ferraris, *Prompta Bibliotheca, Canonica, Juridica, Moralis, Theologica, nec non Ascetica, Polemica, Rubricistica, Historica* (9 vols., Romae, 1885-1899), s. v. "Archivium", I, 405.

30. *Dictionnaire Raisonné de Diplomatique Chrétienne,* s. v. "Archives Ecclésiastiques", col. 89.

31. *Apologia adversus libros Rufini,* Lib. 3, n. 20 — *MPL,* XXIII, 471.

32. Examples of such references during earlier periods are found in the following: Pope Pelagius II (586), Ep. V — Harduin, III, 426; Pope St. Gregory I (590-604), *Registri Epistolarum Libri XIV,* Lib. VIII, Ep. 29—*MPL,* LXXVII, 931: Letter of Pope St. Deusdedit (614) — Harduin, III, 549; Roman Council at the Lateran (649), Actio II — Harduin, III, 727; Letter of Pope St. Nicholas I (866) — Harduin, V, 606, *et al.*

present Vatican archive buildings were erected in 1612.[33] In 1883 Pope Leo XIII opened the Vatican Archives to the scholars of the world for purposes of scientific research.[34]

33. Katterbach, "Archivio e Archivistica" — *Enciclopedia Italiana* (Milano, 1929-1939), IV, 88.

34. Epistola ad Emos. Cardinales Antonium De Luca, Vice-cancellarium S. R. E., Joannem Baptistam Pitra, Bibliothecarium S. R. E., Josephum Hergenroether, tabulariis Vaticanis praefectum ... die XVIII Augusti, MDCCCLXXXIII — *Acta Sanctae Sedis* (41 vols., Romae, 1865-1908), XVI (1883), 49-57.

HISTORICAL DEVELOPMENT

CHAPTER II

DIOCESAN ARCHIVES BEFORE THE SIXTEENTH CENTURY

Before the sixteenth century there seems to have been almost a total lack of ecclesiastical legislation dealing with diocesan archives. In no place do the sources available to the writer reveal that any precise laws were made for their erection by the bishops. What few references to them are found concerning their contents and custody indicate that their existence was taken for granted by the legislators. Nevertheless, that such archives did exist, and that they were in use rather early and quite universally, can be well established.

An indication of diocesan archives is noted in the very early years of the Church. During the first three centuries, when parishes were coextensive with dioceses and the bishops themselves had the direct care of the faithful as pastors,[1] the records of baptisms, called diptychs, were kept in the bishop's house.[2] However, clearer evidence of well-organized archives is brought to light by a consideration of those of the Patriarchal See of Constantinople, which were especially well known because of the position of honor that Church held in the East. Because of their importance they are here treated separately.

A decree of the Council held at Sardica in 343 referred to the archives of Constantinople when describing how certain heretical writings had been deposited in these archives to keep them from falling into the hands of the faithful and corrupting them.[3] After relating several matters connected with the discipline of the Church of Alexandria, the Patriarch Acacius of Constantinople wrote to Pope St. Simplicius (ca. 475) informing the Holy Father that correspondence between a former bishop of Alexandria and the Holy See had been found in the archives of Constantinople.[4] Various epistles of the Monothelite heretics, which constituted the subject-matter for a great

1. *Thomassinus,* Pars I, Lib. II, cap. 21, n. 4.

2. Catalanus, *Rituale Romanum Benedicti XIV,* I, 32; II, 344, in O'Rourke, *Parish Registers* (Washington, 1934), p. 21.

3. Harduin, I, 672.

4. Harduin, II, 805.

part of the proceedings of the III General Council of Constantinople (680), were at certain times taken from the archives of the Patriarchal See and presented to the Council by Georgius, *chartophylax* and deacon.[5] In the IV General Council of Constantinople (869) mention is made of the symbols of faith being kept *"in chartophylacio venerabilis patriarchae."*[6] There is an indirect reference made to the archives of Constantinople in a letter of Anastasius, Archivist (*Bibliothecarius*) of the Holy See, to Pope Hadrian II (867-872).[7]

But besides those at Constantinople, archives were maintained also in other dioceses. To settle quarrels among bishops of the African Church over the primatial dignity, which the Council of Mileve (402) decided was to be determined by their seniority in consecration, the bishops of the Province of Numidia, assembled in this Council, prescribed a register showing the dates of consecration. This register, they decreed, as well as the archives of the Numidian Church, was to be located at the Primatial See, and in the Metropolitan City of Constantia.[8]

In the Acts of the Council of Chalcedon (451) a paper was read which had been taken *"ex sacro scrinio libellorum et sacrorum cognitionum."*[9]

At the beginning of the Synod of Carthage (525), Boniface, Bishop of that See, had a letter of the aged Bishop Missor of Numidia read. In this writing the latter requested a copy of the proceedings of the Synod, in order that he might preserve it in his diocesan archives.[10] In this same Synod Boniface requested that the constitutions of the ancient Fathers be brought from the archives of his own Church, that they might be at hand for reference.[11] Later, when Boniface was asked by the bishops present for more definite information on a cer-

5. Actiones XII, XIII, XIV — Mansi, XI, 543, 546, 558, 587.

6. Actio III — Harduin, V, 790.

7. Harduin, V, 756.

8. C. LXXXVI, "Deinde placuit omnibus episcopis, qui in hoc concilio subscripserunt, ut matricula et archivus Numidiae, et apud primam sedem sit, et in metropoli, id est, Constantia." — Mansi, III, 786.

9. Actio I — Harduin, II, 174.

10. Harduin, II, 1074.

11. Harduin, II, 1077.

tain question that had arisen, he again referred to the writings kept in the archives of the Church of Carthage.[12]

At the end of the II Council of Orange (529), the presiding bishop, Caesarius of Arles, ordered authentic copies of the constitutions to be made and deposited in the archives of that diocese.[13]

A meeting of Catholic bishops with Oriental heretics is described by Innocentius, Bishop of Maronia in Thrace, in a letter written in 533 to a certain priest Thomatius. In this meeting the heretics endeavored to show that their doctrines had been taught by St. Cyril of Alexandria, and offered as a proof the writings preserved in the archives of the Alexandrian Church.[14]

In the first canon of the III Council of Paris (557) the bishops were instructed in the manner of dealing with those persons who had usurped church property, and the canon concluded with the observation that it would not be fitting if the bishops came to be regarded merely as the guardians of the documents through which this property was deeded to the Church, and not as the protectors of the property itself.[15]

The Emperor Justinian (527-565) made rules for ecclesiastical *chartularii,* and designated a certain number for the archives of the various provinces of the empire.[16] He also ordered that the documents of a certain type of marriage be placed in the archives of the "venerable Church."[17]

In a letter written by St. Boniface to Archbishop Nothelm of Canterbury (736), that great missionary requested copies of correspondence carried on between Pope St. Gregory I and St. Augustine of England. St. Boniface remarked that these letters, dealing with the marriage impediment of consanguinity, could not be found in the archives of the Holy See.[18]

12. Harduin, II, 1084.

13. *Monumenta Germaniae Historica, Legum Sectio III, Concilia Aevi Merovingici,* I (Hannoverae, 1893), 53. (Hereafter this work will be referred to as *MGH*).

14. Harduin, II, 1163.

15. Harduin, III, 337.

16. C. (1. 2.) 25.

17. N. (74. 4.) 2.

18. *MPL,* LXXXIX, 739.

Anastasius, *Bibliothecarius* at Rome, wrote to Pope John VIII (872-882) informing the Holy Father that the decrees of the Council of Constantinople (680) could not be found in the archives of any other patriarchal see than that of Constantinople.[19]

At the Council of Paris (825) there was read to the assembled bishops a communication from Emperor Louis the Pious (814-840). In this communication the Emperor speaks of the *"armarii nostrae sanctae ecclesiae"* containing a letter from Pope St. Gregory I to Severus, Bishop of Marseilles.[20]

In the preface to the capitulary of Benedict the Levite, the writer of that spurious collection called himself a cleric of the Church of Mainz, who had been commanded by his Archbishop, Autgar (825-847), to compose the work from the documents drawn from archives of that archdiocese.[21]

The archives of Mantua were consulted for records of a Council supposedly held in that city in the year 827,[22] and in the latter half of the ninth century the archives of Rheims are mentioned by Archbishop Hincmar of that See, who speaks of the diligence of the *scrinii* or archivists at that place.[23]

In the Constitutions of the Church of Lincoln (1212) there are described the duties of the chancellor, which fact indicates the use of archives in that diocese.[24]

One of the offices of the episcopal cathedral chapters from the eleventh to the fourteenth centuries was that which was held by the

19. Mansi, XII, 983.

20. *MGH, Legum Sect. III, Concilia Aevi Karolini,* II (Hannoverae et Lipsiae, 1906), pars 2, 525.

21. *MGH, Legum Sectio, Capitularia Spuria II* (Hannoverae, 1887), pars 2, 39.

22. *MGH, Legum Sectio III, Concilia Aevi Karolini,* II, pars 2, 584.

23. *Dissertatio Secunda de Praedestinatione,* Cap. XXXVI—*MPL,* CXXV, 391.

24. "Ad Cancellarium autem pertinet litteras capituli et chartas componere, ... libros etiam theologiae ecclesiae custodire, et alios similiter in armariolo conservare, quos singulis annis in prima septimana Quadragesimae coram deputatis ad hos ostendere debet et exhibere ut sic appareat quod nullus fuerit perditus vel deterioratus...."—Wilkins, *Concilia Magnae Britanniae et Hiberniae* (4 vols., London, 1737), I, 536.

scholasticus, to whom was entrusted, among other duties, the work of archivist, because of his personal qualifications.[25]

The custody of these diocesan archives was entrusted to clerics, usually priests[26] or deacons.[27] In the Western Church they were called *chartularii,*[28] *scrinii*[29] and *bibliothecarii,*[30] while in the East they were known as *chartophylaces.*[31] In his notes on the IV General Council of Constantinople (870) Anastasius described the power and dignity with which the office of guardian of the archives was endowed.[32]

The causes for the absence of any precise legislation on diocesan archives during this long period cannot be established with any certainty. However, some possible reasons may be suggested. In the first place, the careful attention that was evidently given to archives, at least during the first nine centuries, may have precluded the necessity of such definite laws. Some of the foregoing references to the archives of the various sees reveal the fact that, whenever documents in these archives were called for, they were easily available and quickly pro-

25. Cf. Schneider, Philipp, *Die Entwicklung der bischoeflichen Dom Kapitel bis zum vierzehnten Jahrhundert* (Mainz, 1882), p. 97.

26. Roman Council at the Lateran (649), Actio III — Harduin, III, 798.

27. Council of Constantinople under Mena (536), Actio V — Harduin, II, 1315; III General Council of Constantinople (680), Actio III — Mansi, XI, 543; Johannes Diaconus, *Vita Greg. M.,* Lib. II, c. 55 — *MPL,* LXXV, 115.

28. Johannes Diaconus, *Vita Greg. M., loc. cit.*

29. Hincmar of Rheims, *Dissertatio Secunda de Praedestinatione,* Cap. XXXVI — *MPL,* CXXV, 391.

30. Adnotationes Anastasii Bibliothecarii ad Synodum VIII (870), (IV General Council of Constantinople) — Harduin, V, 942.

31. Anastasius Bibliothecarius, *loc. cit.*

32. "Chartophylax interpretatur chartarum custos. Fungitur autem officio chartophylax apud Ecclesiam Constantinopolitanam, quo bibliothecarius apud Romanos, indutus videlicet insulis ecclesiasticorum ministrorum, et agens ecclesiastico conventui praesentatur; nullius epistola Patriarchae missa recipitur, ac proprie pertinere probantur officium. Sine illo praeterea nullus Praesulum aut Clericorum a foris veniens in conspectum Patriarchae intromittitur; nullus ecclesiastico conventui praesentatur; nullius epistola Patriarchae missa recipitur, nisi forte a caeteris Patriarchis mittatur; nullus ad Praesulatum vel alterius ordinis clericatum, sive ad Praespposituram monasteriorum provehitur, nisi iste hunc approbet et commendet atque de illo ipsi Patriarchae suggerat, et ipse praesentet." — *Loc. cit.*

duced.[33] Mention was made also of the praise that Hincmar of Rheims expressed for the diligence of the archivists of that diocese in the ninth century.[34] Furthermore, in no place in the sources was there to be found any complaint against the manner in which these archives were maintained. On the contrary, those who occupied the position of archivist were held in high esteem, and much authority and dignity were attached to their office.[35]

33. Cf. especially the Synod of Carthage (525) — Harduin, II, 1077 and 1084; III Council of Constantinople (680), Actiones XII, XIII, XIV — Mansi, XI, 543, 546, 558, 587.

34. *Dissertatio Secunda de Praedestinatione,* Cap. XXXVI — *MPL,* CXXV, 391.

35. Cf. Anastasius' testimony in footnote above, p. 15.

CHAPTER III

DIOCESAN ARCHIVES FROM THE SIXTEENTH CENTURY TO THE PUBLICATION OF THE CODE

Considerable legislation dealing directly with diocesan archives is found during the period extending from the latter part of the sixteenth century to the publication of the Code of Canon Law. It was very detailed and comprehensive. Specific laws were enacted commanding the *erection* of episcopal archives in many dioceses, and regulating such matters as their *contents, custody* and *use*. One of the reasons for this sudden appearance of clear provisions can be traced to the evident neglect which was current among not a few of the bishops in preserving and safeguarding important documents. While of course it cannot be said that this negligence was universal,[1] yet it was widespread and extended over a long period of time. This is revealed by the prefaces to some of the laws, wherein such carelessness and indifference are deplored by the legislators.[2] But worse than the neglect during this period were the serious abuses whereby many documents were actually changed, stolen and destroyed. Pope St. Pius V gave as his reason for addressing a constitution[3] to the bishops of Sicily the existence of such conditions in that country. Besides, the severe *penalties* with which he and almost all subsequent legislators sanctioned their laws regarding the custody of diocesan

1. For example, the Provincial Council of Benevento (1693), Tit. XV, Cap. II, commends the archives of the Metropolitan See, holding them up as a model of care, order and thoroughness in archive maintenance. — *Acta et Decreta Sacrorum Conciliorum Recentiorum, Collectio Lacensis* (7 vols., Friburgi Brisgoviae, 1870-1890), I, 39.

2. Benedict XIII, constitution "*Maxima vigilantia,*" June 14, 1727—*Bullarium Romanum,* XXII, 560, *Fontes,* n. 293; Plenary Council of the Bishops of Ireland at Thurles (1850) — *Coll. Lac.*, III, 793; III Plenary Council of Baltimore (1884) — *Acta et Decreta Concilii Plenarii Baltimorensis Tertii,* A. D. MDCCCLXXXIV (Baltimorae: John Murphy, 1886), n. 271, p. 155; Plenary Council of Sydney (1885) — *Acta et Decreta Concilii Plenarii Australasiae habiti apud Sydney* (Sydney, 1887), p. 89.

3. "*Muneris nostri,*" March 1, 1571 — *Bullarium Romanum,* VII, 893.

documents, indicate the seriousness of the situation and the anxiety of those in authority to correct these evils.[4]

With but two minor exceptions[5] none of the legislation pertaining to diocesan archives during these four centuries was of a general nature, for it was promulgated only for particular provinces or dioceses. The enactments of some places, however, had a marked influence upon laws made elsewhere. In many cases they were not only cited as sources, but their very words were adopted to express later provisions for far distant dioceses.[6] Most influential were the constitutions of the Roman Pontiffs, even though they were not universal in scope. Of the three that appeared during this period, the first, the "*Muneris nostri*" of Pius V (March 1, 1571),[7] had provisions concerning the custody of diocesan archives and penalties for their violation, which were repeated in many councils celebrated after its publication.[8] The laws of Sixtus V, promulgated in his constitution "*Provida*" (April 29, 1587)[9] for the dioceses of Italy, commanding the erection of archives and the drawing up of inventories of ecclesiastical property, are found in nearly all subsequent legislation. But the most complete and precise statement on this subject up to the time of the Code was

4. These penalties will constitute the subject-matter of a special article in this chapter. Cf. *infra,* p. 36.

5. Decretum S. C. Ep. et Reg., 16 oct. 1600—*Fontes,* n. 1586; Benedict XIV, const. "*Satis Vobis,*" Nov. 17, 1741—*Fontes,* n. 319.

6. Compare, for example, the Council of Toledo (1565), Pars III, Decr. 1—Harduin, X, 1158, 1159, with the Council of Mexico (1585), Lib. III, Tit. VIII—Harduin, X, 1676-1677; also the Council of Naples (1699), Tit. XII, Cap. II, n. 10—*Coll. Lac.,* I, 238, with the Council of Mount Lebanon (1736), Pars III, Cap. V, n. 10—*Coll. Lac.,* II, 332.

7. *Bullarium Romanum,* VII, 893-894.

8. Examples are: Council of Benevento (1693), Chap. IV—*Coll. Lac.,* I, 40; Council of Naples (1699), Tit. III, Cap. II, n. 12—*Coll. Lac.,* I, 239; Council of Rome (1725), Cc. III, IV, V—*Concilium Romanum in Sacrosancta Lateranensi Basilica Celebratum, Anno Universalis Jubilaei, MDCCXXV* (Bruxellis, 1726), pp. 40, 41, 42; Council of Fermo (1726), Tit. VI—*Coll. Lac.,* I, 594; I Council of Halifax (1857), Decr. XIX, n. 8—*Coll. Lac.,* III, 755; Plenary Council of the Bishops of Ireland at Thurles (1850), Decr. XXI—*Coll. Lac.,* III, 793.

9. Quaranta, *Summa Bullarii Earumve Summorum Pontificum Constitutionum* (Venetiis, 1622), s. v. "Archivus", p. 88.

the constitution "*Maxima vigilantia*" of Benedict XIII (June 14, 1727),[10] addressed to the ordinaries of the dioceses of Italy and the adjacent islands. So thoroughly and clearly is the matter treated in this work, that it has not only been the model for much local legislation since its appearance,[11] but it has, to a great extent, been the foundation for the very canons of the Code itself.

Article 1. Erection of Diocesan Archives

Although some of the legislators who made provisions for diocesan archives during this period presupposed that such archives were already in existence, most of these provisions specifically commanded their erection by the bishops. They differed, however, in assigning the location of the archives. In most cases freedom was given to the bishops in choosing the place for their erection. Some, following the example of Pope Sixtus V, who first used the expression in his constitution "*Provida*," April 29, 1587,[12] simply employed the indeterminate phrase "in a safe and convenient place."[13] Even when a place was suggested, this legal direction was sometimes followed by such words as "or any other place selected by the bishop because of its convenience." Such liberty was granted by the Councils of Toledo (1566)[14] and of Mexico (1585).[15] But both these Councils had provided that the archives were to be located in some monastery within the episcopal

10. *Bullarium Romanum,* XXII, 560-567.

11. For example, Council of Mount Lebanon (1736), Cap. V, nn. 2 and 10 — *Coll. Lac.,* II, 330 and 332; Plenary Council of the Bishops of Ireland at Thurles (1850), Decr. XXI — *Coll. Lac.,* III, 793; I Council of Halifax (1857), Decr. XIX, n. 8 — *Coll. Lac.,* III, 755; III Plenary Council of Baltimore (1884) — *Acta et Decreta Concilii Plenarii Baltimorensis Tertii,* n. 271, p. 155.

12. Quaranta, *Summa Bullarii,* s. v. "Archivus", p. 88.

13. Benedict XIII, const. "*Maxima vigilantia,*" June 14, 1727, n. 2 — *Bullarium Romanum,* XXII, 560; Council of Fermo (1726), Tit. VI — *Coll. Lac.,* I, 595; Council of the Bishops of Ireland at Thurles (1850), Decr. XXI — *Coll. Lac.,* III, 793; Plenary Council of the Bishops of Sydney (1885) — *Acta et Decreta Concilii Plenarii Australasiae habiti apud Sydney,* p. 89.

14. Actio III — Harduin, X, 1159.

15. Lib. III, Tit. VIII, n. V — Harduin, X, 1677.

city. Later, however, the Sacred Congregation of the Council, in permitting the Bishop of Astorga to erect diocesan archives in any safe place he would choose, forbade their erection in convents and monasteries.[16] Other councils required bishops to maintain an archive in common with the cathedral chapters, or also with the collegiate chapters, for preserving records of the administration of the ecclesiastical property of their dioceses, and to establish this common archive in the cathedral or also the collegiate churches.[17] This arrangement may have been the source of the dispute settled by the Sacred Congregation of the Council in 1704, which Congregation allowed the Bishop of Astorga to preserve documents pertaining to the *mensa episcopalis* in his own archives, despite an immemorial custom, claimed by the cathedral chapter, of keeping such papers in the archives of the chapter.[18] In some places the archives were to be set up in the episcopal palace.[19] The Council of Mount Lebanon (1736) mentions the cathedral church as the location for all diocesan archives.[20]

There are a few references to the erection of secret diocesan archives before the appearance of the Code. Although not explicitly designating them as such, the III Provincial Council of Milan (1573)[21] and the Council of Ravenna (1885)[22] had provisions ordering bishops to re-

16. S. C. C. *in Astoricen.*, 12 ian. 1704—Pallottini, *Collectio Omnium Conclusionum et Resolutionum Quae in causis propositis apud Sacram Congregationem Cardinalium S. Concilii Tridentini Interpretum Prodierunt ab ejus institutione anno MDLXIV ad annum MDCCCLX, distinctis titulis alphabetico ordine per materias digesta* (Romae, 1868-1893), s. v. "Archivium," n. 62, Vol. II, p. 506. (Hereafter this collection will be cited simply as Pallottini).

17. I Provincial Council of Milan (1565), Const. LXII—Harduin, I, 696; Council of Toulouse (1590), Pars IV, Cap. III, n. 11—Harduin, X, 1821.

18. S. C. C. *in Astoricen.*, 12 ian., 1704—Pallottini, s. v. "Archivium", n. 8, Vol. II, p. 498.

19. Council of Naples (1699), Tit. XII, Cap. II, n. 6—*Coll. Lac.*, I, 237; Council of Rome (1725), Tit. XII, Cap. III—*Concilium Romanum*, p. 40; Benedict XIII, const. "*Maxima Vigilantia*," June 14, 1727, n. 2—*Bullarium Romanum* XXII, 560; S. C. C. in *Viterbien.-Tuscanen.*, 14 sept., 1782—Pallottini, s. v. "Archivium", n. 60, Vol. II, p. 506.

20. Pars III, Cap. IV, n. 37—*Coll. Lac.*, II, 329.

21. Decr. XVIII—Harduin, X, 795.

22. Pars IV, Cap. IX, n. IX—*Coll. Lac.*, VI, 211.

serve a special place in their archives for the documents of their diocesan courts, which place was to be locked with two keys, one to be held by the bishop and the other by the chancellor. These special precautions in the light of their similarity to the present law in canon 379, § 3, indicate that secret archives were desired. The same inference may be drawn from the enactment of the Council of Mexico (1585),[23] which stated that after the bishop's death the vicar-general was to take all the processes and books from the *camera* (the bishop's financial office) and deposit them in the general archives.

In the catalogues of the writings which the Council of Benevento (1693)[24] and the Council of Rome (1725)[25] required bishops to preserve in their archives, there are listed all the acts and writings pertaining to matters of the Holy Office, which were to be kept in a separate archive, locked with a key. Secret archives were expressly commanded by Pope Benedict XIV for records of marriages of conscience and of baptisms of children born from such marriages, which records he wished to be deposited *"in secretiori loco"* of the episcopal chancery.[26] The Diocesan Synod of Lucca (1887) used the same phrase when referring to documents that demanded a more careful custody.[27] Speaking of the yearly reports which, when furnished by the rural deans were to be preserved *"in secreto tabulario episcopali"*, the Plenary Council of Latin America (1898) naturally presupposed that such secret archives were already in existence.[28] Finally, Pope Pius X, in prescribing rules for the four offices to be established for the administration of the Vicariate of Rome, ordered the erection of two archives, one secret and one non-secret.[29]

23. Lib. III, Tit. VIII, n. VI — Harduin, X, 1677.

24. Title XV, Appendix 5 — *Coll. Lac.*, I, 103.

25. *Concilium Romanum*, Appendix II, Chap. 3, n. 9, p. 232.

26. Encyclical Letter, "*Satis Vobis*," Nov. 17, 1741, §§ 10, 11, 14 — *Fontes*, n. 319.

27. *Lucanae Ecclesiae Synodus Dioecesana* (Lucae, 1887), p. 308.

28. *Acta et Decreta Concilii Plenarii Americae Latinae in Urbe Celebrati, A. D., MDCCCXCIX* (Romae, 1902), n. 851, p. 375.

29. Const. "*Etsi Nos*," Jan. 1, 1912 — *Fontes*, n. 697.

Article 2. Contents of Diocesan Archives

In wording the legal provisions concerning the contents of diocesan archives, some of the legislators used quite general terms. They commanded bishops, for example, "to guard in the most secure manner, all the writings pertaining to their episcopal office, its rights and its transactions",[30] or to preserve "inventories of ecclesiastical property . . . and all documents of major importance pertaining to all the churches of the dioceses",[31] or, again, to keep records of "all matters pertaining to the diocese, and lest any original documents be lost, copies are to be made by the Archivist."[32] The III Plenary Council of Baltimore (1884) stated that "all documents pertaining to diocesan business, both spiritual and temporal", were to be kept in the archives.[33]

Most of the laws were more specific, and in some cases very detailed. The I Provincial Council of Milan (1565) ordered the preservation of the records of ordinations,[34] and the II Provincial Council of that same Province (1569) required a book recording all papal bulls received by the bishops.[35] The Council of Rouen (1581) mentioned records of ordinations, of appointments to benefices and of all other acts emanating from the bishops or their vicars-general,[36] and the Council of Mexico (1585) all briefs and privileges of Roman Pontiffs, all letters and provisions of the King, and all other writings pertaining to the episcopal dignity and jurisdiction.[37]

A lengthy list of documents which were to be preserved was recounted in a letter sent by the Sacred Congregation of the Council, under the date of November 25, 1625, to the Vicar of Perugia. In it were enumerated documents pertaining to ecclesiastical things, such

30. Council of Toledo (1565-1566), Pars III, Decr. I — Harduin, X, 1158.
31. Council of Fermo (1726), Tit. VI — *Coll. Lac.*, I, 595.
32. I Council of Halifax (1857), Decr. XIX, n. 8 — *Coll. Lac.*, III, 755.
33. *Acta et Decreta Concilii Plenarii Baltimorensis Tertii,* n. 271, p. 155.
34. Const. IX — Harduin, X, 656.
35. Tit. I, Decr. V — Harduin, X, 736.
36. *De Jurisdictione Ecclesiastica,* n. 9 — Harduin, X, 1255.
37. Lib. III, Tit. VIII, n. IV — Harduin, X, 1676.

as synods, matrimonial cases, and church property; those relating to sacred places, such as churches, seminaries, cemeteries, monasteries and the like; documents of ordinations, benefices, confessors, religious professions and other matters connected with ecclesiastical persons; and, finally, documents of ecclesiastical courts. This list, referred to by the same Sacred Congregation in 1773,[38] is given in full by Pignatelli.[39]

Another letter of the Sacred Congregation of the Council, reproduced by Ferraris[40] and said to have been written December 18, 1626, to

38. S. C. C. *in Sutrina,* 23 ian. 1773 — Pallottini, s. v. "Archivium", n. 71.

39. *Consultationes Canonicae* (Coloniae Allobrogum, 1700), Consult. 210, n. 4, Tom. IV, p. 360 — "Processus, et facta similia [civilia], criminalia, et mista [mixta] facta in foro Episcopali. Sententiae in eisdem causis latae. Compositiones cum reis inquisitis in Curia Episcopali. Praecepta, et decreta quaecumque inter personas ecclesiasticas, aut etiam laicos in causis, et negotiis spiritualibus, vel alias ad forum ecclesiasticum pertinentibus. Statuta, et Ordinationes Ecclesiarum. Mandata procurae pro gerendis negotiis Episcopatus. Scripturae multarum [mulctarum], et poenarum. Item supplicationum et absolutionum. Acta Synodi. Visitationes Ecclesiarum, monasteriorum, et piorum locorum, eorumque decreta. Registra Bullarum Apostolicarum ad eandem Curiam directa. Collationes, et institutiones beneficiorum, eorumque concursus, et renunciationes, ac permutationes, et scripturae omnes beneficiales. Instrumenta traditionis professionis eorumdem beneficiorum. Uniones beneficiorum. Erectiones parochialium beneficiorum, Cappellarum, et fontis baptismalis. Acta cognitionum Canonizationum, patronatus tam Clericorum, quam laicorum, seu mistorum [mixtorum]. Scripturae concernentes executionem dispensationum matrimonialium, et aliarum litterarum Apostolicarum. Remissiones denunciationum, divortia, et aliae scripturae matrimoniales. Explorationes voluntatum novitiarum, licentiae profitendi et aliae hujus generis scripturae ad monasteria Monialium spectantes. Interpositiones auctoritatis, et decreti in reunuciatione novitiorum, et alienationibus aliarum personarum fori Episcopalis, et instrumenta monialium. Licentiae accedendi ad monasteria monialium, aut in ea ingrediendi. Scripturae consecrationis Ecclesiarum, altarium, coemeteriorum, campanarum, et hujusmodi. Item professionis fidei. Item scripturae visitationis Liminum. Scripturae ordinationis, et collationis Chrismatis. Monitoria ad finem revelandi. Approbationes confessariorum, et Curatorum. Dimissoriae, et commendatitiae. Licentiae pro Parochis, Canonicis, et aliis Clericis, abscedendi e dioecesi cum litteris testimonialibus. Scripturae erectionis, et institutionis seminarii. Item locationis in emphytheusim bonorum Episcopatus, et aliorum bonorum ecclesiasticorum."

40. *Prompta Bibliotheca,* s. v. "Archivium", n. 13, I, 405.

the Bishop of Como, likewise contained an enumeration of the documents that were to be kept in diocesan archives. This letter was referred to and used as a source by later legislators. It was cited by the Council of Benevento (1693),[41] which reproduced it in a more orderly arrangement in an appendix to the acts of the Council.[42] The Council of Rome (1725) also mentioned this letter, and although it completely changed the order of listing the various documents, almost verbatim gave a translation of it in Italian.[43] Since the wording of this second letter of the Sacred Congregation, as it is given by Ferraris, is substantially identical with that of the earlier letter to the Vicar of Perugia, it may safely be concluded that the Bishop of Como simply received a copy of the other.

The Council of Naples (1699) ordered the following to be preserved in the archives: documents of all processes, criminal, contentious, matrimonial, beneficial and spiritual; catalogues of all indulgences and of the relics kept in the churches of the diocese; inventories of all goods, movable and immovable, belonging to churches and ecclesiastical benefices; pious legacies and their documents; bulls of abbacies, dignities, canonicates and of any other benefice; and all

41. Title XV, Chap. III — *Coll. Lac.*, I, 39.

42. Title XV, Appendix V. There were a few substantial differences, however. The Council omitted "acta . . . patronatus," and "Scripturae . . . collationis Chrismatis," but added "Acta et Scripturae concernentes fundationem Ecclesiarum, altarium, Locorum piorum, cum fundationum instrumentis; Decreta quae in causis alienationis bonorum ecclesiasticorum interponuntur; Omnia Inventaria bonorum stabilium, mobilium, etc., omnium Ecclesiarum et Locorum Piorum Civitatis et totius Dioecesis." — *Coll. Lac.*, I, 103.

43. *Concilium Romanum*, Appendix XI, p. 229. — This Council likewise made some additions to the list. "Tutti gli Statuti, Regole, ed Ordinanzioni di qualunque Chiesa, Capitoli, e Collegi nelia [nella] Città, e Diocesi. Tutte le Scritture delle soppressioni di Parrochie, Benefizi, o Cappellanie. Tutti gli Atti, et Scritture, appartenenti a materie di S. Offizio, che devono conservarsi in Armario a parte, chiuso a chiave. Tutte le Platee, ed Inventari de' beni stabili, mobili, semoventi etc. di tutte le Chiese, e di tutti i Luogi pii della Città, e della Diocesi. Tutti i Mandati di procura pergli negozi della Mensa Vescovile, e gli Strumenti spettanti alle dote, o a' beni della Medesima Mensa. Tutte le Scritture di Enfiteosi, Locazioni, e conduzioni de' beni della Mensa Vescovile. Cosi anche degli altri Benefizi, Chiese, e Luoghi pii. Tutti gli Editti fatti in qualunque modo, ed in qualsisia materia, col registro de esse in libro."

rights pertaining to the ecclesiastical forum and especially to the *mensa episcopi.*[44]

In the East the various records were preserved by inscribing them in books kept by the chancellor. Such books had notations of professions of faith, ordinations, visitations of churches and dispensations.[45] There were other books recording confirmations, consecrations of churches, altars and cemeteries; books of ecclesiastical trials, sentences, censures, absolutions and of all other matters decided by the bishop or his vicar in civil and criminal cases; books containing inventories of churches, documents and privileges of the church, authentic documents of relics, legacies, donations and other rights belonging to the cathedral; finally, rituals, pontificals and ecclesiastical books pertaining to the celebration of the Divine Office or to the *jus dicendum.*[46]

Besides those documents which were required by almost all the later councils of this period, such as records of ordinations, testimonial letters, matrimonial dispensations, appointments to benefices and the erections and divisions of parishes, mention is made of preserving annotations of the names of the priests working in the dioceses,[47] documents pertaining to the origin and history of the dioceses, privileges granted to churches by diocesan authorities,[48] edicts,[49] written reports of episcopal visitations, formularies of oaths signed by a priest being incardinated, records of the quinquennial examinations of the junior clergy, financial reports of mission churches,[50] transfers and

44. Tit. XII, Cap. II, n. 7 — *Coll. Lac.*, I, 238.

45. Council of the Ruthenians, Greek Uniate Rite (1720), Tit. VIII — *Coll. Lac.*, II, 52.

46. Council of Mount Lebanon (1736), Pars II, Cap. V, n. 2 — *Coll. Lac.*, II, 329.

47. IV Provincial Council of Baltimore (1840), Decr. IX — *Coll. Lac.*, III, 71.

48. Plenary Council of the Bishops of Ireland at Thurles (1850), Decr. XXXI, n. 2 — *Coll. Lac.*, III, 793; Plenary Council of Sydney (1885), *Acta et Decreta Concilii Plenarii Australasiae habiti apud Sydney*, n. 265, p. 89.

49. Council of Ravenna (1885), Pars IV, Cap. IX, n. IX — *Coll. Lac.*, VI, 211.

50. III Plenary Council of Baltimore (1884) — *Acta et Decreta Concilii Plenarii Baltimorensis Tertii*, nn. 14 and 64, pp. 188 and 272.

removals of rectors, administrators and assistants, and finally, acquisitions or alienations of ecclesiastical property.[51] Special solicitude was shown regarding any documents that would insure the safe passage of this church property into the hands of a bishop's or a superior's successor in the United States. A decree of the Sacred Congregation for the Propagation of the Faith (December 15, 1840) stated that, in parts of this country where corporations could not be legally formed, bishops to whom property was given for ecclesiastical or pious uses were to make wills leaving this property to one of their fellow bishops. Copies of these wills were to be placed in the archives of the Metropolitan See. Superiors of religious institutions were to draw up similar wills, leaving the property to their successors, and copies of these wills were to be deposited in the diocesan archives.[52] In accordance with this decree some of the Councils of Baltimore held after that date enacted the called-for legislation.[53]

Among the provisions in the laws of that time there were some which are similar to those now stated in the Code, commanding that inventories of, or, in some cases, copies of the documents kept in the files of churches, confraternities or pious places, be sent to the diocesan archives.[54] Besides the inventories of ecclesiastical property, required by almost all legislators, the pastors or other superiors were ordered to transmit to the chanceries records of lay confraternities,[55] statements showing the receipts of foundations, together with an inventory of the documents expressing the wishes of the founders,[56] copies of baptism

51. IV Provincial Council of New York (1883) — *Acta et Decreta Concilii Provincialis Neo-Eboracensis Quarti, MDCCCLXXXIII* (Neo-Eboraci, 1886), Art. II, p. 69.

52. *Fontes*, n. 4786.

53. V Provincial Council of Baltimore (1843), Decr. I — *Coll. Lac.*, III, 89; II Plenary Council of Baltimore (1866) — *Acta et Decreta Concilii Plenarii Baltimorensis II*, n. 191, p. 115; III Plenary Council of Baltimore (1884) — *Acta et Decreta Concilii Plenarii Baltimorensis Tertii*, n. 269, p. 154.

54. Canon 383, § 1.

55. Council of Mount Lebanon (1736), Pars IV, Cap. IV, n. 13 — *Coll. Lac.*, II, 390.

56. Council of Paris (1849), Tit. III, Cap. VIII — *Coll. Lac.*, IV, 25.

records,[57] of marriage and burial records, as well as records of First Holy Communion and Confirmation,[58] and deeds of church property.[59] The Council of Bordeaux (1850) prescribed that when a pastor had died, the vicar-forane, or, in his absence, the oldest pastor of the district, was to draw up an inventory of all the parish records and send it to the bishop.[60]

Concerning the arrangement of these documents in the diocesan archives, hardly any specific rules were made. The system of filing seems to have been left to the choice and the discretion of the bishops. Only such expressions were used as "each document being arranged in its proper place and separated in a fitting order,"[61] "documents are to be deposited in an orderly manner,"[62] "archives are to be strong, spacious and orderly,"[63] "documents are to be arranged methodically in their files,"[64] and "suitably arranged."[65]

No doubt custom was followed in this matter. This is suggested by the Diocesan Synod of Lucca (1887), which specified that the filing of documents was to be according to a certain method employed by one of the earlier archbishops of that See. The explanation given of this method may serve as an example of systems in use, at least during the last century. Each writing was to be numbered in a progressive series, care being taken, however, that all letters pertaining to the same

57. I Provincial Council of Milan (1565), Pars II, n. II — Harduin, X, 648; Council of Toulouse (1850), Decr. LXIV — *Coll. Lac.,* IV, 1053; Council of Aix (1850), Tit. VII, Cap. II, n. 8 — *Coll. Lac.,* IV, 989.

58. Council of Aix (1850), *loc. cit.*

59. IV Provincial Council of Baltimore (1840), Decr. VIII — *Coll. Lac.,* III, 71; Council of English, Dutch and Danish Colonies in the East Indies (1867), Decr. Sect. II, n. 10 — *Coll. Lac.,* III, 1114.

60. Tit. IV, Cap. VIII, n. 8 — *Coll. Lac.,* IV, 586.

61. Council of Naples (1699), Tit. XII, Cap. II, n. 6 — *Coll. Lac.,* I, 237.

62. Council of Rome (1725) — *Concilium Romanum,* Tit. XII, Cap. III, p. 40.

63. Benedict XIII, const. *"Maxima vigilantia,"* June 14, 1727, § 2 — *Bullarium Romanum,* XXII, 560; *Fontes,* n. 293.

64. Council of Ravenna (1855), Pars IV, Cap. IX, n. 9 — *Coll. Lac.,* VI, 211.

65. III Plenary Council of Baltimore (1884) — *Acta et Decreta Concilii Plenarii Baltimorensis Tertii,* n. 271, p. 155.

business were collected under the same number. The writings were then to be listed under their proper numbers in the index. Every year the documents were to be placed in a *capsula* (probably a box-like folder), on the back of which was to be inscribed the year to which they belonged.[66]

Article 3. Custody of Diocesan Archives

It is true that during this period the immediate custody of the archives was entrusted to certain persons called secretaries,[67] *custodes archivi*,[68] archivists,[69] or more frequently chancellors.[70] All legislators, however, placed them under the direct care and supervision of the ordinaries, upon whom was laid the responsibility for their custody. This is revealed by the very wording of some of the laws. A decree of the Sacred Congregation of Bishops and Regulars[71] stated that a notary was obliged to send the original documents of a completed trial to the *ordinary,* in order that he might preserve them in his archives. Bishops were to gather, in so far as it was possible, all documents pertaining to their office and to the affairs and rights of their churches, and place them in the archives.[72] With all diligence they were to gather and restore letters and documents of legacies and foundations, which notaries had not as yet returned through forgetfulness or carelessness.[73] They were to inquire after all docu-

66. *Lucanae Ecclesiae Synodus Dioecesana,* p. 308.

67. Council of Rouen (1589), *De Jurisdictione Ecclesiastica,* n. 9—Harduin, X, 1255.

68. Council of Naples (1699), Tit. XII, Cap. II, n. 10—*Coll. Lac.,* I, 238.

69. Benedict XIII, const. "*Maxima vigilantia,*" June 14, 1727, § 23—*Bullarium Romanum,* XXII, 566; *Fontes,* n. 293.

70. Council of the Ruthenians, Greek Uniate Rite (1781), Tit. VIII—*Coll. Lac.,* II, 52; Diocesan Synod of Ferrara (1781)—*Synodus Dioecesana Ferrariensis, MDCCLXXXI* (Ferrariae, 1781), n. XVI, p. 273; Council of Urbino (1859), Decr. CXXVII—*Coll. Lac.,* VI, 43; III Plenary Council of Baltimore (1884)—*Acta et Decreta Concilii Plenarii Baltimorensis Tertii, A. D. MDCCCLXXXIV,* n. 271, p. 155.

71. Oct. 16, 1600, § 11—*Fontes,* n. 1586.

72. Council of Benevento (1693), Tit. XV, Cap. I—*Coll. Lac.,* I, 38.

73. Council of Avignon (1725), Tit. XLVI, Cap. I, n. II—*Coll. Lac.,* I, 579.

ments that had been removed from the archives or mislaid, and to use any remedies necessary to have them restored, or at least to have it revealed where they were hidden.[74] Besides, they were to visit the archives every two years, in the presence of a notary and two witnesses.[75]

It is quite evident, too, that this obligation, imposed so directly upon the bishops, was regarded as grave. The Council of Toledo (1565), for example, observed that bishops should be mindful of the oath taken by them at their consecration not to alienate church property; but that they would be guilty of such alienation, if, through their negligence in keeping the archives, the very documents which protected the goods and the rights of the church should be lost.[76]

The archives were to be locked at all times and the archivist could never give the keys to anyone.[77] Benedict XIII ordered two different keys, one to be kept by the ordinary and the other by the chancellor or a notary of the curia.[78] He also provided that documents pertaining to trials were to be transmitted by notaries and actuaries to the archivist within one month[79] after the completion of a case. When archivists or other custodians of documents were changed, they were obliged by means of public document to notify their successors of all the writings contained in the archives. Otherwise both they and their successors would be held liable for missing documents.[80]

74. Benedict XIII, const. "*Maxima vigilantia,*" June 14, 1727, § 18 — *Bullarium Romanum,* XXII, 564; *Fontes,* n. 293.

75. Council of Toledo (1565), Actio II, Decr. I — Harduin, X, 1158; Benedict XIII, const. "*Maxima vigilantia,*" June 14, 1727, § 13 — *Bullarium Romanum,* XXII, 563; *Fontes,* n. 293.

76. Actio III, Decr. 1 — Harduin, X, 1159.

77. Council of Naples (1699), Tit. XII, Cap. II, n. 10 — *Coll. Lac.,* I, 238; Council of Mount Lebanon (1736), Pars III, Cap. V, n. 10 — *Coll. Lac.,* II, 332; Benedict XIII, const. "*Maxima vigilantia,*" June 14, 1727, § 2 — *Bullarium Romanum,* XXII, 560; *Fontes,* n. 293; Diocesan Synod of Lucca (1887) — *Lucanae Ecclesiae Synodus Dioecesana,* p. 308, n. 1.

78. "*Maxima vigilantia,*" § 10 — *Bullarium Romanum,* XXII, 562; *Fontes,* n. 293.

79. The Council of Mount Lebanon (1736) allowed two months — Pars III, Cap. V, n. 10 — *Coll. Lac.,* II, 332.

80. "*Maxima vigilantia,*" § 23 — *Bullarium Romanum,* XXII, 565; *Fontes,* n. 293.

The Sacred Congregation of the Council decreed that all documents of the episcopal forum were to be preserved in the chancery of the bishop, and not in the public archives of the city. All such documents that had been sent to the city archives were to be returned to the chancery office.[81] The Diocesan Synod of Ferrara (1781) forbade chancellors to allow letters or books to be taken out of the curia, and stated that if they or any other person possessed books or writings belonging to the curia or the forum, they had to return them within one month.[82]

In another response the Sacred Congregation of the Council advised that the *acta* of a diocese which had been joined to another diocese should be preserved in their proper chancery office, even if they had been drawn up by the chancellor of the other see, and that chancellors were bound to transmit all documents to the chancery office of the diocese to which they belonged.[83]

Even more careful was the custody of the archives which was required by the legislators during the vacancy of the episcopal see. According to the law of the Council of Toledo (1565), as soon as the bishop had died, the vicar-general was to hand over the two keys of the archives, one to the cathedral chapter, or some person deputed by the chapter to receive it, and the other to the prelate of the monastery in which the archives were located. The latter had to take an oath that he would guard the archives faithfully and allow no document to be removed without the permission of the metropolitan or the metropolitan's superior. When the new bishop was appointed, the chapter and the superior of the monastery were to give him the keys, and submit to him a report of the documents removed from the archives during the vacancy, with an explanation of the reason for their removal. The chapter was obliged also to hand over to him any documents received by the canons during that time.[84] This last pro-

81. S. C. C., *in Sutrina,* 23 ian. 1773 — Pallottini, s. v. "Archivium", n. 71, Vol. II, p. 508.

82. *Synodus Dioecesana Ferrariensis,* n. XVI, p. 273.

83. S. C. C., *in Viterbien. seu Tuscanen.,* 11 ian. 1783 — Pallottini, s. v. "Archivium," nn. 66 and 67, Vol. II, p. 506.

84. Actio III, Decr. 1 — Harduin, X, 1158.

vision was a restatement of the law of the Council of Trent.[85] Almost verbatim is the whole law repeated in the Council of Mexico (1585).[86]

The II Provincial Council of Milan (1569) ruled that during the vacancy one of the two keys was to be kept by the vicar capitular, the other by one of the canons chosen by reason of office, custom or seniority. When they delivered the keys, they had to render an account to the new bishop of all the documents that had been committed to their care.[87]

Among the Oriental Rites it would seem that the chancellor was in charge of the archives during the vacancy, for it was he who was ordered to give the books and documents to the new bishop.[88]

Benedict XIII wished the keys to be retained by canons deputed by the chapter. He added that for no reason could they give them to another, not even to the Apostolic *Commissario* (a special judge delegated by the Holy See). The latter was only permitted the privilege of examining any document to the inspection of which he was entitled in view of his commission, but in the presence of the canons who held the keys. Nor could he remove such documents, because of the obligation resting upon the chapter to give an account of all the documents to the new bishop.[89] Later councils protected the archives of a vacant diocese in a similar manner. When a bishop foresaw his death approaching, he was to name in his will two priests to whom custody of the archives was to be entrusted after his death.[90]

A special means used by the legislators to insure safe custody of the documents in diocesan archives consisted in the demand of having accurate inventories drawn up. Not only were these ordered to be

85. Sess. XXIV, *de ref.*, c. 16 — Harduin, X, 163.

86. Lib. III, Tit. VIII, n. VI — Harduin, X, 1677.

87. Tit. III, Decr. XIV — Harduin, X, 795.

88. Council of the Ruthenians, Greek Uniate Rite (1720), Title VIII — *Coll. Lac.*, II, 52; Council of Mount Lebanon (1736), Pars III, Cap. V, n. 2 — *Coll. Lac.*, II, 330.

89. Const. "*Maxima vigilantia,*" June 14, 1727, § 21 — *Bullarium Romanum*, XXII, 565; *Fontes*, n. 293.

90. Council of the Bishops of Ireland at Thurles (1850), Decree XXI, n. 3 — *Coll. Lac.*, III, 793; Plenary Council of Sydney (1885) — *Acta et Decreta Concilii Plenarii Australasiae habiti apud Sydney* (1885), n. 266, p. 90.

compiled, but strict and detailed regulations were enacted to safeguard their preservation. The Councils of Toledo (1565)[91] and of Mexico (1585)[92] provided for a carefully made inventory of all writings signed by the bishop or the vicar-general and a notary, which was to be kept with the documents. Pope St. Pius V required inventories for documents of trials.[93] The Council of Naples (1699) commanded inventories of all documents and of the grants of rights, and insisted that they be kept up to date.[94] The Council of Rome (1725) ordered that each year an inventory of all the processes of the episcopal curias and of all the documents in the archives was to be drawn up, and that the bishops were to preserve these carefully.[95]

In the detailed instructions of Benedict XIII, ordinaries were obliged to have inventories and catalogues made by the chancellor or a notary, who would sign each page. These were to give a brief synopsis of each letter and document. When completed, the whole catalogue was to be examined by the ordinary, who would show his approval of it by himself signing it at the end.[96] Each year a catalogue of the writings of the previous year, as well as of older ones that had been overlooked, was to be added.[97]

The Diocesan Synod of Lucca (1887) took even greater precautions. It stated that the priest in charge of the archiepiscopal archives should make an index of all documents contained therein, and the chancellor in charge of the curial archives should do the same. Two priests, appointed in the Synod, were to compare the inventories with the documents to see if they agreed, and having made out a duplicate report, they were to present one to the archbishop and place the other in the archives. Each year in the month of January these deputies together with the vicar-general were to visit the archives and again compare the documents with the indexes, and if anything was out of

91. Actio III, n. 1 — Harduin, X, 1158.
92. Lib. XXX, Tit. VIII, n. IV — Harduin, X, 1676.
93. *"Muneris nostri,"* March 1, 1571 — *Bullarium Romanum,* VII, 893.
94. Tit. XII, Cap. II, n. 8 — *Coll. Lac.,* I, 238.
95. *Concilium Romanum,* Tit. XIII, Cap. V, p. 42.
96. Benedict XIII, const. *"Maxima vigilantia,"* June 14, 1727, § 5 — *Bullarium Romanum,* XXII, 561; *Fontes,* n. 293.
97. *Ibidem,* § 12.

order, they were to report it to the archbishop. The inventories were to be kept up to date, which fact the deputies and the chancellors had to attest by their signatures.[98]

Just as for the archives themselves, so also a more particular custody was commanded for the inventories when a see was vacant. Pope St. Pius V ordered that when a bishop foresaw his death approaching, the inventory was to be sealed and given to the priest to whom he confessed his sins. After the bishop's death, this priest was to turn it over to the prelate of the most important monastery of the city, who was to guard it faithfully until he delivered it, with seal unbroken, to the new bishop.[99] The Council of Naples (1699) repeated this law, but instead of specifying that this inventory should be entrusted to the confessor or religious superior, the Council simply ordered that the inventory be left with a dependable man.[100] This same regulation was adopted by the Council of Rome (1725), which added, however, that the bishop should also leave the inventory with the superior of the monastery whenever he anticipated a long absence from his diocese.[101] This addition was included also in the provision of the Council of Fermo (1726), which further stated that when the bishop had died, the canons of the cathedral chapter, who succeeded to the ordinary jurisdiction, together with the vicar-general of the deceased bishop, were at once, if possible even before the election of the vicar capitular, to visit the archives and the chancery office, prepare a new inventory, and deposit it with the one the bishop had left.[102] In his constitution Pope Benedict XIII similarly made special provision for meeting the particular needs occasioned either by a bishop's absence or by his death. He added, moreover, that in each transfer of the inventory a receipt was to be given by the person receiving the inventory, and this receipt was not to be returned to the holder of the inventory until the inventory had been delivered to the returning bishop or the newly installed bishop. The Pope also stated that if the confessor or religious

98. *Lucanae Ecclesiae Synodus Dioecesana*, p. 309.

99. "*Muneris nostri,*" March 1, 1571 — *Bullarium Romanum,* VII, 893.

100. "*. . . probatae fidei viro.*" — Tit. XII, Cap. II, n. 9 — *Coll. Lac.*, I, 238.

101. *Concilium Romanum*, Cap. IV, p. 41.

102. Tit. V — *Coll. Lac.*, I, 595.

superior should die before he had delivered the inventory to the proper bishop, then such a confessor's or religious superior's confessor was to take the inventory and assume the same responsibilities of guarding and transmitting it, for it became his duty to carry out the tasks which the deceased penitent had not been able to fulfill.[103]

Very precise is this Holy Father's instruction about the custody of the inventory after the bishop's death. Before a vicar capitular was elected, the canons of the cathedral chapter were to seek out the inventory most diligently, and ascertain whether or not it had been given to the proper confessor. If it had, the canons were to take it and deliver it to the regular superior of the monastery. If it was not found, and at the same time it was clear that it had never been given to the confessor, then two of the older canons were to take the keys of the archives, and in the presence of two priests who were not canons they were to seal the outside of the archives with their own seals, so that the archives could not be opened with the keys. Neither the other canons nor the vicar capitular could break the seal or open the archives. The archives were only to be opened by the two older canons in the presence of two priests who were not canons. The two canons were then to compare the documents with a second authentic inventory, which was also commanded by this constitution to be preserved in the archives. Should this second inventory be missing, the two canons were then to have a duplicate inventory of the documents made by a public notary, one copy of which was to be placed in the archives, and the other delivered to the superior of the monastery.[104]

Article 4. Use of Diocesan Archives

In order to avoid abuses or carelessness, the safeguarding of certain conditions was required in the removal of documents from the archives or in their presentation for use by persons not connected with the chancery offices.

The Council of Toledo (1565) decreed that no original document could be removed except for a grave reason connected with the bish-

103. *"Maxima vigilantia,"* § 19 — *Bullarium Romanum,* XXII, 564.
104. *Ibidem,* § 20.

op's duties or for some cause beneficial to the Church. If such a reason did exist, the documents could be removed, provided this were done in the presence of a notary and two witnesses. The notary was to record the removal in the inventory, together with the date, the name of the person taking the document and the purpose for which it was taken.[105] The archivist or actuary of a case still pending, who had loaned documents with the proper permission, was to obtain receipts for them and to take care that the documents were returned within fifteen days. In the same law the Council declared that original documents could be given only to ecclesiastical persons of the city or diocese, and that the permission of the vicar-general for this had to be given in writing.[106]

Most stringent was the regulation of the Council of Ravenna (1568). It forbade under any circumstances the loaning of documents to anyone, even to the representatives of the bishop or to the cathedral chapter, and even when one would promise on his word of honor to return them or would give security for them.[107]

The V Provincial Council of Milan (1579) forbade chancellors and notaries to show the original documents of trials to anyone unless this were done in their own office or in the place where the documents were located. Such original documents, however, could never be taken away, except when they had to be shown to the judge in a trial. Copies of the documents could be given only with the written permission of the vicar-general.[108] In the Council of Naples (1699) similar laws prohibited any person from examining documents except in the presence of the archivist, and the latter was forbidden to furnish any copies of the documents without the permission of the vicar-general.[109]

According to Pope Benedict XIII's constitution, no papers could be removed from the archives without the written permission of the ordinary. After three days these writings were to be returned to their proper places, where receipts were held against the person who had

105. Again the Council of Mexico (1585) adopted the same legislation. Cf. Lib. III, Tit. VIII, n. IV — Harduin, X, 1676.

106. Actio III, n. 1 — Harduin, X, 1158.

107. Cap. 4 — Mansi, XXXV, B, 607.

108. Pars III, Const. XIV — Harduin, X, 1084.

109. Tit. XII, Cap. II, n. 10 — *Coll. Lac.*, I, 238.

taken the writings until such time as he returned the documents. The receipts furnished by the person when he borrowed the writings or documents had to be signed in his own handwriting in a book kept for this purpose in the archives. Local ordinaries, however, had the faculty of proroguing this time, but only moderately.[110] This provision is repeated in a response of the Sacred Congregation of the Council.[111]

More lenient in the matter of time for the duration of which documents could be borrowed was the legislation of the Council of Mount Lebanon (1736) which determined that bishops could loan documents from the archives, but for no longer than fifteen days.[112]

The Diocesan Synod of Lucca (1887) stated that documents of any kind were not to be shown by the archivist to anyone without the permission of the bishop or of the vicar-general. Even with the permission of the one or the other of these, the documents could be read only in his presence. Under no circumstance could they be taken away.[113]

Article 5. Penalties for Violating the Laws Concerning Diocesan Archives

The laws concerning diocesan archives which were enacted during the four centuries prior to the appearance of the Code, especially the laws which dealt with the custody of the documents, were usually sanctioned with canonical penalties. In some instances these punishments were very severe. In their development over this period can be seen the foundation for the censure and the vindictive penalties stated in the Code for offenses of this kind.[114]

To check the abuses of his time, Pope St. Pius V threatened the loss of dignity, office or benefice to anyone guilty of removing or destroying documents pertaining to criminal trials.[115] This ruling of the Sovereign Pontiff was to have a definite influence in the shaping of

110. *"Maxima vigilantia,"* June 14, 1727, § 22 — *Bullarium Romanum,* XXII, 565; *Fontes,* n. 293; cf. canon 378.

111. S. C. C., *in Placentina Iurium Parochialium,* 25 maii, 1816 — Pallottini, s. v. "Archivium", n. 39, Vol. II, p. 501.

112. Pars III, Cap. V, n. 10 — *Coll. Lac.,* II, 332.

113. *Lucanae Ecclesiae Synodus Dioecesana,* p. 308.

114. Canons 2405 and 2406.

115. Const. *"Muneris nostri,"* March 1, 1570—*Bullarium Romanum,* VII, 893.

subsequent legislation of this nature. Without change or addition it was adopted by the Council of Benevento (1693).[116] But most of the laws that restated it annexed certain further provisions. The Council of Rome (1725) included under the same punishment, besides the principal agents committing such acts, all those clerics whose guilt of participation was reflected in their aid, counsel or bribery.[117] The same law was repeated in the Council of Fermo (1726), which in addition threatened certain penalties for guilty laymen.[118] Its influence extended even to the middle of the nineteenth century, when it was incorporated in the laws of the Council of the Bishops of Ireland at Thurles (1850)[119] and of the Council of Halifax (1857),[120] both of which also stated the punishment of excommunication to be *ipso facto* incurred by laymen for these misdeeds.

The V Provincial Council of Milan (1579) decreed that one who took original documents of trials from the archives was to be punished by the bishop with grave penalties, and that such a person was bound to repair any damage that might arise from this act. It further stated that a chancellor or a notary who would give copies of these documents to anyone was to be deprived of his office and was obliged to suffer any other punishment that the bishop might see fit to inflict.[121]

According to the Council of Mexico (1585), one who at the time of the bishop's death hindered the vicar-general from transferring the processes and books of the bishop's office (which were kept in the bishop's own archives) to the general diocesan archives was to be punished with a major *latae sententiae* excommunication; and if it was a chapter or a community which put such an obstacle in the way

116. Title XV, Chap. IV — *Coll. Lac.*, I, 40.

117. *Concilium Romanum*, Title XI, Chap. V, p. 42.

118. Tit. VI, "Quodsi laicus fuerit, gravibus poenis pecuniariis vel corporis afflictivis, etiam damnationis ad Triremes, pro modo culpae coerceatur, et praeter has externi fori poenas, nemo sacerdotum audeat illum absolvere absque speciali Episcopi licentia (quae in generali casuum reservatorum concessione comprehensa non intelligatur) et facta prius eo modo, quo fieri poterit, reintegratione." — *Coll. Lac.*, I, 596.

119. Decree XXI, n. 4 — *Coll. Lac.*, III, 793.

120. Tit. XIX, n. 8 — *Coll. Lac.*, III, 755.

121. Pars III, Const. XV — Harduin, X, 1084.

of the performance of this duty by the vicar-general, then that group became subject to ecclesiastical interdict.[122]

Similarly strict were the sanctions found in the Council of Naples (1699), which provided that one who took documents from the archives or gave them to another was to be punished with formal imprisonment and with other penalties according to the judgment of the bishop.[123] This Council likewise imposed a *latae sententiae* excommunication upon anyone who effaced, burned, suppressed or hid processes, documents or writings pertaining to the curia, the forum or the income of the bishop.[124] This penalty is also stated in the Council of Mount Lebanon (1736).[125] The same punishment was likewise incurred by one who at the time of the Council had an original document in his possession and failed to return it within two months.[126]

The laws of the Diocesan Synod of Ferrara (1781) ordained that whoever would dare to hide, destroy, tear or deface a writing belonging to the diocesan archives, no matter who he might be, was subject to excommunication; he could not be absolved from it until the writing was returned or repaired. Then he was to undergo whatever other penalties the bishop in his discretion might decide to impose.[127]

The penalties invoked by Benedict XIII to give force to his provisions for diocesan archives were, as was to be expected, the most detailed of all this penal legislation. After observing that his whole constitution[128] bound in virtue of holy obedience all those who were subject to its enactments, he declared that ordinaries who violated its rulings were to be suspended from the use of the *Pontificalia*, according to the judgment of the Holy Father. On cathedral and collegiate chapters the laws were imposed under pain of interdict; on other secular clerics, under pain of suspension *a divinis;* on regulars of either sex, under pain of suspension from office and the loss of active

122. Lib. III, Tit. VIII, n. VI — Harduin, V, 1677.

123. Tit. XII, Cap. II, n. 10 — "... *sub poena carceris formalis aliisque ad arbitrium.*" — *Coll. Lac.*, I, 238.

124. *Ibidem*, n. 12.

125. Pars III, Cap. V, n. 10 — *Coll. Lac.*, II, 332.

126. *Loc. cit.*

127. *Synodus Dioecesana Ferrariensis*, n. XVII, p. 274.

128. "*Maxima vigilantia,*" June 14, 1727, § 25 — *Bullarium Romanum*, XXII, 566.

and passive voice in elections; on laymen, under pain of major excommunication. Besides these general punishments, the same constitution stated that vicars capitular and canons of cathedral chapters who neglected the constitution's provisions for the custody of diocesan archives when the see was vacant, or who at that time presumed to open the sealed archives, were to sustain whatever financial loss had been occasioned by their act, and besides, were to be subject to any other penalties the new bishop might inflict.[129] Over and above the general punishments, too, archivists who failed to draw up the prescribed inventories of documents pertaining to trials, were to be deprived of their office, and rendered perpetually incapable of resuming it.[130]

Just as all the other pre-Code legislation which dealt with diocesan archives was particular in its scope, so also there were no penal laws which pertained to this subject in the nature of a general application. Not even in the constitution "*Apostolicae Sedis*" of Pope Pius IX (Oct. 12, 1869), which restated many of the penalties enacted for various crimes up to that time, is there any mention of a punishment being imposed for negligence or abuses in connection with episcopal archives.[131]

129. *Ibidem*, § 20.
130. *Ibidem*, n. 23; *Fontes*, n. 293.
131. *Fontes*, n. 552.

CANONICAL COMMENTARY

INTRODUCTION

In the Code of Canon Law the Legislator recognizes the importance of episcopal archives for diocesan administration. The article on this subject embraces ten canons[1] and lays down rules for the erection of both common and secret archives, their contents, custody and use.

This first general law of the Church concerning diocesan archives confirms the more detailed provisions promulgated by Pope Benedict XIII for Italy and the adjacent islands,[2] and extends many of them throughout the whole Church. Indeed, so closely does the present law follow the legislation contained in that constitution, that some of the canons are expressed in the very phrases used by Pope Benedict.[3]

Although some of the canons mention only residential bishops, all of the obligations stated in this article apply also to other ordinaries who rule over territories constituted in the manner of dioceses. Canon 304, § 1, expressly imposes these laws on vicars and prefects apostolic and canon 323, § 1, generically upon abbots and prelates who govern autonomous independent territories (*abbates et prelati nullius*).[4]

1. Cc. 375 to 384.

2. Const. "*Maxima vigilantia,*" June 14, 1727 — *Bullarium Romanum,* XXII, 560-567; *Fontes,* n. 293.

3. Compare, for example, "*Maxima vigilantia,*" § 2, with canon 375, § 1; "*Maxima vigilantia,*" § 5, with canon 375, § 2; "*Maxima vigilantia,*" § 12, with canon 376, § 1; "*Maxima vigilantia,*" § 18, with canon 376, § 2; and "*Maxima vigilantia,*" § 22, with canon 378.

4. These ordinaries were also included by Pope Benedict XIII in the above-cited constitution, § 2 — *Bullarium Romanum,* XXII, 560; *Fontes,* n. 293.

CHAPTER IV

GENERAL OR COMMON DIOCESAN ARCHIVES

Article 1. Erection and Contents

Can. 375, § 1: Episcopi in loco tuto ac commodo archivum seu tabularium dioecesanum erigant, in quo instrumenta et scripturae, quae negotia dioecesana tum spiritualia tum temporalia spectant, apte dispositae et diligenter clausae custodiantur.

A. *The Erection of Archives*

Bishops are expressly commanded to erect archives in a safe and suitable place. The evident purpose of the Lawgiver in enacting this law, especially his desire to preserve the more important documents belonging to the Church, supports Toso in his conclusion that this canon expresses a grave precept.[1]

As the canon suggests, the choice of a place for the erection of diocesan archives should be given the most careful consideration. The most appropriate location would seem to be within the building in which the various offices of the diocesan curia are situated.[2] It is desirable, too, that a separate room be used for the archives. This room should not be selected at random, much less because it is unfit for any other purpose.[3] For example, to relegate diocesan records to dark and dirty attics or damp cellars would not be to provide a safe and suitable place as the canon demands. Even when the small size of a chancery building will not allow a separate room for the archives, the place chosen must be so prepared as to meet these requirements of safety and suitability.

1. *Ad Codicem Iuris Canonici Commentaria Minora* (Romae: Ephemeridis Ius Pontificium Cura et Impensis, 1925), Liber II, *De Personis*, Pars I, Tomus III, p. 22.

2. Wernz-Vidal, *Ius Canonicum*, 7 tom. in 8 vols., Vol. II (Romae, Apud Aedes Universitatis Gregorianae, 1923), n. 647.

3. Rozman, "Cerkveno arhivno pravo" — *Bogoslovni Vestnik*, IV (1924), 148.

The place will be safe if it is so constructed and the archives are so arranged in it that protection against theft, fire and dampness is assured, and danger of damage to the documents from any other cause is removed.[4] Many of these dangers can be eliminated by employing modern resources such as steel, stone, concrete and asbestos in the construction of a new building,[5] and in older structures the archive room could be rebuilt with similar materials.

To safeguard the archives against theft the doors to the room should be heavier than the average door. Wooden doors could be reënforced by an inside door of metal bars, or the heavy steel vault doors could be used, as they are in some chanceries. The door, no matter of what kind, must be fortified with a strong lock. The combination locks on vault doors will meet the requirements of safety demanded for the protection of the archives, for the chancellor can guard the combination just as carefully as a key.[6] It is true that against the use of this type of lock the objection may be raised that the combination, if entrusted to another during the absence of the chancellor, can be retained in memory and made use of on later occasions. The objection, however, is not so strong as to cause any serious difficulty. In the first place the person to whom the temporary custody of the archives is given will naturally be chosen with care and discretion; and even if, in spite of this fact, such a person should be actually so dishonest as to wish to betray his trust, he would also be able to have a duplicate key made while the original key to the archives is in his possession. The objection, therefore, considers only a most extraordinary circumstance. Yet in the matter of safeguarding the archives, all that can be required of the bishop is that he exercise that diligence which is employed by the average prudent man; and combination locks are used quite extensively by administrators and are generally regarded as a suitable means of protecting documents and valuables. Besides, the combinations to such locks can easily be changed, and it is the practice of some officials to renew the combinations periodically, for example, once or twice each year. The windows of the archive room should also be protected

4. Cf. Wernz-Vidal, *Ius Canonicum,* II, n. 647.

5. Jenkinson, *A Manual of Archive Administration* (2. ed., London: Percy Lund, Humphrey & Co. Ltd., 1937), p. 46.

6. Cf. canon 377, § 2.

by iron bars or by a steel rolling shutter, which can be pulled down and fastened when no one is to be present in the room.

To avoid the danger of fire the archives must not be placed in contact with or near easily inflammable substances. Electric wiring for lighting the room should be properly fused and insulated. It would be circumspect to provide in advance by the designation of some fixed plan which will lend itself serviceably as a definite and efficacious means of removing the contents of the archives quickly and expeditiously whenever a fire should break out. As a fundamental aid for the realization of this plan it will be practical to provide a fire-escape close to the window of the archive room or to have a stairway-exit near the door which leads from the room to the outside of the building.[7]

The danger to documents from water is normally much greater (under modern conditions) than from fire.[8] Special precautions, therefore, should be taken to keep the archive room as dry as possible. Water dripping from the ceiling and windows or from a defective heating system which could cause moisture, should especially be guarded against. If possible no water pipes should lead through any part of the room from which a leakage would cause damage to the contents of the archives.

Other natural enemies of documents in archives, such as rats and mice, insects and larvae, can be combated to a great extent by insisting on absolute cleanliness of the room at all times. The danger from wood-worm can be eliminated entirely by using steel cases and shelving instead of wooden ones.

The Code requires that the place for the diocesan archives, in addition to being safe, be suitable or convenient. It must, therefore, be large enough to accommodate, and in an orderly arrangement, *all* the documents and writings that the bishop will find it necessary or expedient to preserve. Adequate space should be allowed also for working in comfort, for a desk and a chair and for whatever other furnishings may be needed. The room should be well heated and sufficiently ventilated and lighted. Not only are these conveniences required for the health of those who must work in the room, but they are necessary

7. Rozman, "Cerkveno arhivno pravo", *Bogoslovni Vestnik,* IV (1924), 148.
8. Jenkinson, *A Manual of Archive Administration,* p. 46.

for the preservation of the documents themselves. Air is considered one of the best preservatives of parchment and paper, and light is likewise valuable.[9]

The archive room should be conveniently located in the chancery building so that a means of easy access is afforded to the officials of the various offices whose records are kept in the archives. Likewise it should be close enough to the chancellor's office to enable him to have the vigilance over the archives that his position demands.[10] A telephone connection for communication with the various offices is both practical and advisable.

While the Code does not distinguish between a current and a stationary archive, it seems to suppose such a division[11] when it prescribes that at the beginning of each year the archives are to be complemented by depositing in them inventories of the documents and writings of the preceding year.[12] In this division current archives are maintained in each of the separate offices of the chancery under the supervision of the chancellor, but at certain times, for example, once a year, as the above canon suggests, or as often as local regulations direct, their contents are transferred to the stationary archives in a common archive room. Such a system is very commendable in that it keeps at hand for each official the more recent documents to which innumerable references must be made in the course of a working day, and it likewise provides for their safer custody whenever the writings become less needed. It also affords a more convenient use of the correspondingly less crowded current files. It is employed in many chanceries in the United States.

In the erection of the archive itself uniformity in shape and size should be sought as much as possible. Not only neatness in appearance but also efficiency in the use of the archives makes this desirable.

9. Cf. Jenkinson, *A Manual of Archive Administration,* p. 47. This author warns, however, that "it is not wise to expose documents too much to the direct rays of the sun, because of their possible effect in 'fading' the ink or warping the parchment or paper."

10. Canon 372, § 1.

11. Cf. D'Angelo, *La Curia Diocesana a norma del Codice di Diritto Canonico* (Giarre, Sicilia: Pietro Lisi, 1922, p. 95.

12. Canon 376, § 1.

Fortunately, today the size of letters and documents has become so standardized that such uniformity can easily be obtained.

The most practical form of archive is the steel filing cabinet used almost universally in modern office administration. These cabinets are manufactured in two convenient sizes, the larger being called legal or "cap" size and the smaller being designated as letter-size, corresponding to the two most common dimensions of the paper which they are to store. Perhaps the most usual form of cabinet consists of four compartments or drawers, equal in size and one above the other, but some may be purchased having fewer or more drawers, or constructed with the compartments divided into smaller sections to accommodate such materials as index cards or documents folded into smaller but standard dimensions, as insurance policies or deeds to property.

It is filing cabinets such as these, with the number and size of the drawers adapted to the needs of the office which they are to serve, that are recommended for the current archives of the chancery office. The larger or legal-size cabinet is suggested, for while it can conveniently hold the letter-size papers, it will at the same time accommodate the larger ones without any necessity of folding them. Those cabinets which have a lock at the top to secure all the drawers when it is fastened, will best be in keeping with the provisions for the custody of the archives.[13]

It is true that in the repository, or stationary archive, the same type of filing cabinet may be used, but the containers known as transfer cases have the advantage of conserving space. These are also made of steel and in sizes corresponding to the drawers of the filing cabinets, but they are in single compartments, and can be arranged in order on steel shelving, which can be built up to the ceiling against the walls of the archive room.

B. *The Contents*

This canon does not determine in particular which documents and writings are to be kept in the episcopal archives, but merely states in

13. Canon 377.

the generic phrase that their contents are to be "documents[14] and writings pertaining to the spiritual and temporal affairs of the diocese". In other canons, however, the Code mentions specifically certain writings that must be deposited in the diocesan archives. These are copies of the inventories of the writings preserved in the archives of churches, confraternities and pious places;[15] authentic copies of parochial books;[16] the books containing records of ordinations and all the documents pertaining to each ordination;[17] documents attesting to the fact of the consecration or blessing of a sacred place;[18] copies of the inventories required of administrators of ecclesiastical goods;[19] authentic copies of the documents and instruments upon which the property rights of the Church are based;[20] copies of the charters of certain non-collegiate ecclesiastical institutions;[21] copies of the documents establishing pious foundations;[22] and all the documents of a completed ecclesiastical trial which must remain with the tribunal.[23] Obviously these are very few of the documents to be preserved. It would be quite impossible to give an exhaustive list of all the letters and documents which come into or emanate from a chancery office. For a more detailed enumeration, however, it may be helpful to refer to that given above, which was drawn up by the Sacred Congregation of the Council in 1625.[24]

For the greater part, then, it is left to the bishop to decide which of all the documents and papers handled in his chancery office are to be deposited in the archives. These documents and papers necessarily

14. The *instrumenta* are those documents which are drawn up for establishing future proof of anything. Cf. Blat, *Commentarium Textus Codicis Iuris Canonici*, II (Romae: 1921), n. 411; Sipos, *Enchiridion Iuris Canonici* (Pecs: 1926), p. 262.

15. Canon 383, § 1.

16. Canon 470, § 3.

17. Canon 1010, § 1.

18. Canon 1158.

19. Canon 1522.

20. Canon 1523, n. 6.

21. Canon 1490.

22. Canon 1548.

23. Canon 1645, § 2.

24. Chap. III, Art. 2, p. 23.

fall into three groups: writings which come into the office, copies of the writings which go out, and papers which do neither but which circulate within.[25] In the last group would be included, for example, records compiled in the office itself for its own uses, and memoranda of telephone conversations or other verbal proceedings, the knowledge of which must be retained. The canon gives the bishop the norm to follow in making his selection when it states that those are to be preserved "which pertain to the spiritual or temporal affairs of the diocese". Here it may be well to point out one of the principal purposes of archives, which is to assist the administrator in his work, to be, as it were, "a convenient form of artificial memory,"[26] and an authentic evidence of the facts and events of his administration. Archives are not maintained, therefore, in the interest of or for the information of posterity.[27] Though the archives which the bishop is forming may later offer valuable information to historians, this thought should never be the motivating reason for preserving a writing. Rather, he should consider only whether or not the writing pertains to the business of the diocese, and whether it will, in the archives, enable him to carry on his work more efficiently. This criterion will help him to avoid the two extremes either of cluttering up the archives with irrelevant material or of destroying papers and documents which are truly valuable or useful. It may be added that since it is the bishop who is responsible for the writings kept in the diocesan archives, he alone should determine whether or not a paper or document is to be preserved or destroyed.

A complete centralization in the episcopal archives of all the documents and writings pertaining to the whole diocese would be not only impractical, but perhaps even impossible, and it is clear that this is not intended by the Legislator. Canon 383, § 1 definitely provides for other smaller archives, namely, of churches, confraternities and pious places, and in the canons cited above requiring certain records of these moral persons to be sent to the chancery office, only inventories or copies, and not the original documents or records, are demanded.

25. Cf. Jenkinson, *A Manual of Archive Administration*, p. 23.

26. Jenkinson, *op. cit.*, p. 23.

27. Jenkinson, *op. cit.*, p. 11.

Article 2. Arrangement of Documents in Diocesan Archives

Canon 375, § 1 orders that the contents of diocesan archives be "suitably disposed". Indeed an unarranged collection of papers could never fulfill the purpose for which archives are intended. So important is a practical arrangement for the proper use of archives that Ferretti calls it the condition *sine qua non* of an office or an archive.[28]

It would be most difficult, however, to establish one definite system of arrangement which could satisfactorily serve every diocese. Dioceses are so different in size and in other circumstances, and the general contents of their archives are so varied, that to attempt to prescribe a standard system of arranging the documents is almost impossible. It is true that the Code, when stating the principal duties of the chancellor, prescribes a chronological order.[29] But most authors who consider this question are agreed that this does not exclude the employment of other systems. Prümmer, for example, remarks that nothing hinders the use of a systematic order[30] and D'Angelo states explicitly that no fixed rule is laid down. Accordingly the latter author, while considering a chronological order the easiest and most practical for arranging the documents of the current archives, allows any system to be used for the stationary archives.[31] Augustine states that the documents may be indexed according to the names of parishes, or topically, according to subject-matter.[32] Coronata suggests that the arrangement be determined by the ordinary, either in or out of a diocesan synod.[33]

It would seem, then, that any order of arrangement which is definite and workable may be used, and that the choice is entrusted to the

28. Ferretti, *I piccoli archivi ecclesiastici e le piccole biblioteche, riordinati secondo il Codice di diritto canonico e i principali sinodi diocesani* (Roma, 1918), p. 4, apud D'Angelo, *La Curia Diocesana*, p. 95.

29. Canon 372, § 1.

30. *Manuale Iuris Canonici* (3. ed., Friburgi Brisgoviae: Herder & Co., 1922), Q. 133, p. 180.

31. *La Curia Diocesana*, pp. 98-99.

32. *A Commentary on Canon Law* (8 vols., Vol. II, 5. ed., St. Louis: Herder, 1928), 407.

33. *Institutiones Iuris Canonici*, I, n. 428.

prudence of the bishop,[34] and the ingenuity of the chancellor.[35] Certainly they would know better than others the circumstances of their own offices and the suitability of any particular system of filing. In most cases, to obtain a practical arrangement, all that they will require is a knowledge of some sound theory combined with common sense and a little experience. Although, as has been said, it is impossible to formulate rules to cover all individual cases, a method of arranging the documents in diocesan archives is here presented, which, *mutatis mutandis,* may serve as a guide for chanceries in which a new or more satisfactory system is desired.

The first logical division of the documents and writings of the episcopal archives is that made according to the various offices of the diocesan chancery. Any function of the bishop's administration of which the amount of business is great enough to require a special office, is worthy of its own archives. Pope Pius X so divided the archives of the Vicariate of Rome when he established four distinct offices in that curia.[36] Separate archives may be maintained, therefore, for the diocesan tribunal, the offices of diocesan charities, diocesan schools and of missionary activities, and for any other episcopal charge needing an office apart from the general office of the bishop.

The arrangement of the contents of these archives will depend upon the nature of the work handled by each office. Thus in one office they may be arranged alphabetically and in another chronologically, while some documents may better be disposed according to subject-matter. Most offices, however, will require a combination of two or more methods of filing. Perhaps it will serve to clarify this point if some examples are given.

The first office to be considered, and naturally the largest, is the general office of the bishop. The work of this office embraces a multiplicity of the bishop's duties; so in a manner similar to that in which the episcopal archives were first divided to accommodate the special offices in the chancery, the documents of the general office may be separated into categories suggested by the various functions to which they pertain, and a like rule adopted, namely, that every function

34. Canon 375, § 1.

35. Canon 372, § 1.

36. Constitution *"Etsi Nos,"* Jan. 1, 1902, n. 77 — *Fontes,* n. 697.

which has archive material of considerable enough quantity should be given its own classification and assigned a separate compartment in the archives. With such differentiation, certain of these classifications will normally be found in the archives of every diocese, such as Holy See, Apostolic Delegation, Priests, Ecclesiastical Students, Religious, Institutions, Financial Affairs, Deeds, Dispensations, Miscellaneous Clergy, Miscellaneous Laity and many others. In those dioceses where no special office is maintained for the Diocesan Tribunal, Diocesan Charities, Schools, Missionary Activities, etc., the archives of the general office will necessarily include the documents belonging to these functions and will be classified accordingly. Some dioceses, of course, may need space for many other categories of the bishop's work and surveillance, such as the Confraternity of Christian Doctrine, Men Religious as distinguished from Women Religious, Insurance, Banks, Catholic Youth Organization, etc. In every diocese it will be helpful to set aside a special drawer for such records as those of Confirmations, Consecrations and Blessings of Churches, Episcopal Visitations, Financial Recapitulations, Ordinations or others which may have to be consulted or compiled on sudden notice.

As a general rule the contents of these compartments will be arranged alphabetically. With regard to those classified according to persons, as, for example, Priests, Ecclesiastical Students, Miscellaneous Clergy, Miscellaneous Laity, etc., the order may be determined by the surnames of the persons as they appear on the folders in which the documents are placed. For the drawers containing deeds or folders relating to Parishes, Institutions, Religious Communities and the like, the best arrangement may be first according to the names of the cities or towns in which these places are situated, and then according to the proper titles of the places. Records of marriage dispensations may be filed in one place according to the alphabetical order of the man's name, which will be typed together with that of the woman, on the upper part of the face of each document. The drawer containing Diocesan Records may be arranged according to the categories into which these records are naturally separated.

Within the folders the documents, letters, copies, etc., are placed in chronological order, those of more recent date being on top of the others. However, all writings relating to the same item of business should be fastened together before being put in the folder. When cross references are necessary they can conveniently be made by typing extra copies, or at least memoranda, of the documents in question and depositing them in the other folders to which they may have reference.

An entirely different system of filing, one that is mainly chronological, is suggested for the archives of the diocesan tribunal. The work of this office has a natural division into processes or cases. Normally, criminal processes and non-matrimonial contentious cases are very few. Besides, the records of many of them will not remain in the general archives, but will be deposited among the secret documents. It will, therefore, be quite easy to gather all the documents of each of these cases into a separate folder, mark on the top of the folder the name of the party or parties involved in the process and arrange the cases alphabetically.

The records of matrimonial cases, however, could better be arranged in the following manner. As each new case is presented to the tribunal it is given a number which is next in a consecutive series. The number, together with a letter representing the classification of cases to which it belongs, e. g., M. 25, is inscribed on a folder, in which are inserted all the documents of the process as they are received or drawn up by the court, and the folder is filed in the archives according to its number. The same series of numbers may be continued indefinitely, or, if the number of cases warrants it, a new series may be started each year, in which event the number assigned would be M. 25/39 or M. 25/40, the 39 or 40 designating the year in which the case is presented.

Meanwhile a card index is prepared for this file, and arranged alphabetically according to the surnames of the persons involved in the process. A separate card is made out for each person. Thus, if four people are concerned, e. g., the parties to the marriage (John Jones and Mary Smith) and a former spouse of each of these parties (Catherine Brown and James Green), four cards will be prepared, the first showing the name of Jones at the top with the names of Smith, Brown and Green in that order below it, the second having the name Smith in the first place with the names of Jones, Brown and Green following, etc. Each card, of course, will also indicate the number of the case's folder in the archives. The inclusion on the card of a brief summary of the case and a notation of each document pertaining to the process will allow it to serve as the inventory required by canon 375, § 2.[37]

The arrangement of the documents in the repository or stationary archives should correspond in every respect to that in the current archives. A separate section of the common archive room should be given over to the files of each office, and the cabinets or cases to which the folders are transferred should be classified in the same manner as the filing cabinets of the current archives. However, it will be necessary to inscribe on the face of each cabinet or transfer case in the repository either the years to which the documents belong, or, when the documents are grouped into processes or cases, the numbers of these processes or cases.

It may be useful to move the older archives, and especially those that are inactive, to the higher places in the repository, in order to have the more recent documents convenient for consultation. But some records, however old, must be consulted very frequently, and should not, therefore, be so stored away. An example is that of the records of marriage dispensations. Every year these could be bound in book form with an alphabetical list of the names appearing in the front of the bound volume, and on the back of the cover an inscription of the title (e. g., Dispensations, Except Banns) and the year.

Article 3. Custody

Besides assisting the bishop in the efficient administration of his diocese, diocesan archives also serve another purpose. They preserve from loss or deterioration valuable documents, some of which safeguard spiritual rights[38] or protect temporal rights of the Church and her ownership of property.[39] It is easy to understand, therefore, why the Code, in the canon now being considered, commands that the documents and writings in the episcopal archives be diligently cared for and guarded under lock and key; and why, in the second paragraph of the same canon and in the two canons immediately following,

37. Cf. *infra*, Cap. IV, Article 3, p. 56.
38. Cc. 1010, 1046, 1158, *et al.*
39. Cc. 1301 and 1536, n. 6.

there are found detailed provisions dealing with inventories, the care of the documents and the custody of the archives themselves.

As in other periods of the Church's history,[40] so in the present law the responsibility for this custody rests primarily with the ordinary, with a certain amount of vigilance being required also of the chancellor.

A. *Inventories*

Can. 375, § 2: Omni diligentia ac sollicitudine conficiatur inventarium seu catalogus documentorum quae in archivo continentur cum brevi singularum scripturarum synopsi.

Can. 376, § 1: Quotannis, primo bimestri, inventario seu catalogo illae scripturae adiungantur, quae anno praecedenti confectae vel alias neglectae fuerunt.

The Code wishes an inventory or catalogue of the documents contained in the diocesan archives to be compiled. It is evident from former particular laws[41] that the principal reason for making such inventories is that they may serve as a means of safeguarding the documents. Through them the ordinaries are enabled to keep a record of the contents of the archives committed to their care, to offer proof of the Church's ownership of the documents and to identify those which have been taken away or lost.[42] Consequently, much importance is attached to this episcopal duty by the canon when it states that the inventory must be made "with all diligence and care". The ordinary, then, must see to it that it is compiled, and that this work is done accurately and in a practical manner. He may, however, entrust the actual making of the inventory to the chancellor, vice-chancellor or other notaries.[43] Needless to say, care must also be taken to have the inventory closely guarded.

40. Cf. *supra,* Chapter II, p. 13, Council of Paris (557), and Chapter III, Art. 3, p. 28.

41. Cf. *supra,* Chapter III, Art. 3, pp. 31-34.

42. Cf. D'Angelo, *La Curia Diocesana,* p. 103.

43. Cf. Benedict XIII, const. "*Maxima vigilantia,*" June 14, 1727, § 5 — *Bullarium Romanum,* XXII, 561; *Fontes,* n. 293.

No particular form for the inventory is suggested by the law, so the documents may be listed in a bound book, on sheets of paper or on index cards. If a diocese is very small and its documents are few, any of these forms will be satisfactory. But for the larger chancery offices perhaps the most practical inventory will be that compiled on the index cards,[44] for while the latter can correctly serve the primary purpose of preserving a record of each document, they may also be made to contribute to the scientific use of the archives.[45] This is especially true of the archives of very large dioceses, where even in a short time a great number of documents may accumulate in the folders, and consequently be subject to the deteriorating effect of constant handling, particularly when the exact date of a desired document is not known. In such dioceses, and for the same reason in any diocese, the inventory cards can be used as an index file, which will show the date of the document, and thereby indicate more precisely its location in the folder.

The canon requires in the inventory a brief synopsis of each document. There should be indicated the name of the person with whom the document is concerned, the place or office whence it originated, the date it bears, the nature of the document, namely whether it is an original, a copy or a memorandum, and finally a summary of its contents. The last-mentioned may often be expressed in only a few words, but should never be so brief that the document could not easily be identified. If the inventory is to be used as an index file, it will necessarily include also the classification and year under which the document has been filed in the archives and the markings on the folder in which the document is contained.[46]

The arrangement of the inventory will depend upon the form that has been chosen. If it is a registry book, the simplest manner of listing the documents will be in the chronological order of their dates. If the loose sheets of paper are used for the inventory it is clear that they can readily be inscribed with the same titles and separated into the same classifications as the archives, and the record of the document

44. Rozman, "Cerkveno arhivno pravo", *Bogoslovni Vestnik,* IV (1924), 149.

45. Cf. Coronata, *Institutiones Iuris Canonici,* I, n. 428, 4°, b.

46. Cf. D'Angelo, *La Curia Diocesana,* pp. 101 and 122 for examples.

made under its proper classification. However, when cards are employed with the intention of having the inventory serve as an index, an alphabetical order of the surnames of persons will best determine the arrangement. For this reason the names should appear first on the cards and should be more prominent than the other notations. More than one document pertaining to the same person may be listed on a single card, new cards being made out only when it becomes necessary.

Canon 376, § 1, insists that the inventory be kept up to date when it states that within the first two months of every year[47] the records of documents which accumulated during the preceding year, as well as of those which for any reason have not as yet been listed in the inventory, are to be added. But in order to avoid an excess of work at that time, it would seem better to complete the inventory gradually, in such a way that at the end of the year the task will be reduced to the mere removal to the stationary archives of the inventories of those documents which are then being transferred.[48] However, because through carelessness or error certain documents may not have been properly catalogued, the inventory should be compared with the documents before the transfers are made.[49]

B. *Care of Documents*

Can. 376, § 2: Ordinarii sedulo inquirant chartas et scripturas forte alio distractas atque dispersas; et quaelibet necessaria remedia adhibeant ut eaedem scripturae archivo restituantur.

For different reasons documents belonging in the episcopal archives may never have been deposited in them or may have become separated

47. Pope Benedict XIII allowed only the month of January. Const. "*Maxima vigilantia,*" June 14, 1727, § 12—*Bullarium Romanum,* XXII, 561; *Fontes,* n. 293.

48. Cf. Sipos, *Enchiridion Iuris Canonici,* p. 262; Chelodi, *Ius de Personis iuxta Codicem Iuris Canonici* (2. ed., Tridenti, 1927), n. 202; D'Angelo, *La Curia Diocesana,* p. 123.

49. Coronata, *Institutiones Iuris Canonici,* I, n. 428, 4°, b.

from them. Through inadvertence, for example, many documents may have been left in the current archives of the smaller offices of the chancery long after they should have been transferred to the stationary archives. Some may have been taken out of the office with the bishop's permission but not returned at the proper time. Others may have been withdrawn illegally and may still be located in other places or scattered among various individuals.[50] Since *all* documents pertaining to the bishop's administration must be preserved in the diocesan archives,[51] bishops are commanded to institute a careful search for the missing documents and especially for those that have been taken away. It is true that the chancellor, because of his immediate vigilance over the archives, would be more familiar with their contents, but because the means at his disposal for recovering the missing documents would not be so effective as those available to the bishop, the law imposes the duty directly upon the latter.[52]

How frequently this investigation must be made is not expressly stated. Blat remarks simply that the bishop should attend to it whenever he prudently judges it to be necessary.[53] An opportune time might be when, by local regulation or custom, the documents are transferred to the stationary archives. Should the intervals between the transfers be too long, however, a definite time that is shorter should be set for the investigation, because the longer a document is missing, the more difficult it becomes to trace. The particular legislation of Pope Benedict XIII required that the inquiry be made before the compilation of the inventory, which would be once a year.[54] This is a good norm to follow, but certainly the search should be made at least every five years.

Not only must the missing documents be sought, but the canon demands also that when their whereabouts has been ascertained, the

50. Cf. Rozman, "Cerkveno arhivno pravo", *Bogoslovni Vestnik,* IV (1924), 148.

51. Wernz-Vidal, *Ius Canonicum,* II, n. 647.

52. Cf. Coronata, *Institutiones Iuris Canonici,* I, n. 428, 4°, b.

53. "... opportunitate prudenter capta." — *Commentarium Textus Codicis Iuris Canonici,* II, n. 412.

54. Const. *"Maxima vigilantia,"* June 14, 1727, §§ 12 and 18 — *Bullarium Romanum,* XXII, 561 seq.; *Fontes,* n. 293.

bishop must use every means in his power to recover them. Especially is this true when there is question of the documents having been taken out of the chancery. The means adopted by the ordinary will be suggested by the circumstances of person and place, the degree of fault, the value of the document, etc. For example, if possession of a document has been obtained by legitimate prescription,[55] the bishop may regain the document by purchase. If the document is in the hands of one without fault in any regard, the bishop may perhaps obtain it by simple request. However, should a person, physical or moral, retain a document unlawfully and wilfully, the bishop may resort to penal remedies[56] or even, if necessary, to ecclesiastical punishments.[57]

The obligation of the bishop as expressed in this canon obviously includes also that of using every precaution to preserve in good condition the documents which are actually in the archives. He should insist on their being filed promptly and neatly and subjected to as little handling as possible. If any documents are to be bound outside the office, they should not be sent to the binder without the bishop's permission, and before this permission is granted, the bishop must be assured that those to whom the work of binding is entrusted are in every way dependable. Even the older and inactive files should be inspected periodically, and repairs should be made to the archives and documents whenever they are needed.[58]

C. *Custody of the Archives*

Can. 377, § 1: Archivum clausum sit oportet et nemini illud ingredi liceat sine Episcopi aut Vicarii Generalis et cancellarii licentia.

§ 2: Unus cancellarius illius clavem habeat.

55. Canon 1511, § 2.
56. Canon 2306, nn. 1, 2, 3.
57. E.g., canon 2221; cf. Toso, *Ad Codicem Iuris Canonici Commentaria Minora*, Lib. II, *De Personis*, Pars I, Tomus III, p. 23; Rozman, "Cerkveno arhivno pravo" — *Bogoslovni Vestnik*, IV (1924), 148.
58. Cf. D'Angelo, *La Curia Diocesana*, pp. 103-104.

After commanding the special precaution of making an inventory of the documents in the diocesan archives and the bishop's supervision over their timely filing, the Code provides further for their custody by establishing rules for guarding the archives themselves. The archives must be locked with a key and no one is allowed access to them without first having obtained the proper permission.

This law is very strict, and in a large curia where there are many officials who must consult the archives frequently, it would be most difficult to observe. Of course, as Chelodi points out, in those chanceries which have been in existence for a great number of years any custom which may have been formed in this regard can be followed.[59] Cappello maintains that these officials may reasonably presume the necessary permission.[60] However, nothing in the law seems to bar the possibility of an express permission being granted to such persons, once and for all or for an indefinite period of time, to enter the archives.

The permission that must be obtained is twofold, that of the bishop or vicar-general on the one hand and that of the chancellor on the other. There is no doubt that the chancellor's permission is never sufficient without the bishop's or the vicar-general's.[61] But whether or not the permission of the chancellor is always required is a disputed question. Goyeneche maintains that it is not and that only the license of the bishop is necessary to enter the archives.[62] As his reason for this opinion he cites canon 378, § 1, which gives solely to the bishop or to the vicar-general the authority of allowing documents to be taken away from the archives. He claims that this involves a greater concession than the permission which grants admittance to the archives and therefore implies that since the bishop or the vicar-general can

59. *Ius De Personis,* n. 202, footnote 1; canon 5.

60. *Summa Iuris Canonici in usum scholarum concinnata,* Vol. I (2. ed., Romae: apud Aedes Universitatis Gregorianae, 1932), n. 410.

61. Cf. Toso, *Ad Codicem Iuris Canonici Commentaria Minora,* Lib. II, *De Personis,* Pars I, Tom. III, p. 22; Coronata, *Institutiones Iuris Canonici,* I, n. 428, 4°, b, δ; Goyeneche, *Juris Canonici Summa Principia,* Vol. I (Roma, Tip. Pol. "Cuore di Maria", pro Manuscripto, 1935), p. 324.

62. *Loc. cit.*

alone and without the chancellor grant the greater permission, he can also grant the lesser.[63] But to allow the taking away of a single document for a limited time when a signed receipt must be left, as this same canon 378 demands, could not be regarded as conceding a license even as great as would be that of permitting access to *all* the documents at one time and without such added precautions. Coronata attempts to steer a middle course. In his text he explicitly states that permission of the chancellor is required even after that of the bishop has been obtained,[64] but in the words of a footnote he remarks that the chancellor cannot refuse his permission to one who has previously been granted it by the bishop. It seems most inconsistent, however, to hold that a license must be sought from an official who has no option but that of granting it. While it is true that ordinarily the chancellor will not refuse permission after the bishop has conceded it, it cannot be said that he is unable to do so. It may happen that the bishop or vicar-general has given permission unaware of certain circumstances connected with the party to whom it was conceded, which circumstances, being known to the chancellor, strongly prompt him to refuse. In such an event the chancellor would have to be guided by the grave obligation of guarding the archives which is placed upon him directly by the Code and which he must regard as one of the principal duties of his office.[65] Nor is it quite clear what Toso means when, considering this question, he qualifies the permission of the chancellor by saying that it is required "at least under the authority of the ordinary."[66] Thus, while it is true that in a matter of this kind an immemorial custom may be tolerated,[67] in otherwise attempting to interpret the law more mildly, the clear meaning of its words should never be ignored or forgotten;[68] and in this case it is necessary to

63. *Op. cit.*, I, 324, footnote 7.

64. Coronata, *Institutiones Iuris Canonici,* I, n. 428.

65. Canon 372, § 1. Cf. Blat, *Commentarium Textus Codicis Iuris Canonici,* II, *De Personis,* n. 413; De Meester, *Juris Canonici et Juris Canonico-Civilis Compendium* (Brugis: Desclée, De Brouwer et Si, 1923), II, 191.

66. Toso, *Ad Codicem Juris Canonici Commentaria Minora,* Lib. II, *De Personis,* Pars I, Tom. III, p. 23.

67. Canon 5.

68. Cf. canon 18.

maintain unequivocally with Blat,[69] Ayrinhac[70] and Rozman[71] that permission to enter diocesan archives must be obtained both from the bishop or vicar-general *and* from the chancellor.

How great is the responsibility of the chancellor in the matter of guarding diocesan archives is evidenced by the second paragraph of the presently considered canon, which gives to him exclusively the retention of the key. Unlike the provisions of Benedict XIII, which commanded two different keys, one to be kept by the ordinary and the other by the chancellor or a notary of the curia,[72] the present law requires only one key. The chancellor should guard this key jealously and never give it to anyone. However, for the convenience of those who have permission to enter the archives and who may have to use them whenever he is absent, the key should be kept in a safe place in the office rather than on the chancellor's person, and the place should be known to the bishop and the vicar-general.[73]

When the see is vacant the chancellor must be particularly vigilant in his custody of the archives. Since his office and consequently his responsibility in this regard continue during this time, he should especially guard against the possible dangers to documents which are mentioned in canon 435, § 3. This canon forbids anyone, cleric or lay, and even the vicar capitular (or diocesan administrator), to remove, destroy, hide or change any of the documents of the episcopal archives.[74] The gravity of the penalty imposed by the Code for violations of this prohibition clearly indicates the seriousness of the chancellor's obligation to prevent such abuses. Persons guilty of them incur

69. *Commentarium, loc. cit.*

70. *Constitution of the Church in the New Code of Canon Law* (New York: Blase Benziger & Co. Inc., 1925), n. 175.

71. "Cerkveno arhivno pravo", *Bogoslovni Vestnik,* IV (1924), 151.

72. Const. "*Maxima vigilantia,*" June 14, 1727, § 10 — *Bullarium Romanum,* XXII, 562; *Fontes,* n. 293.

73. Cf. *Pisanae Ecclesiae Sinodus XI, Petro S. R. E. Maffi Archiepiscopo celebrata diebus 29-30 sept. et 1 oct., A. D. MCMXX,* Appendice, "Regolumento per gli Archivi Ecclesiastici", n. 3 — apud D'Angelo, *La Curia Diocesana,* p. 109, footnote.

74. "... nominatim vero Vicarius Capitularis aliique sive de Capitulo sive extranei, clerici aut laici, per se vel per alium prohibentur Curiae episcopalis documenta quaelibet subtrahere vel destruere vel celare vel immutare."

ipso facto an excommunication reserved in a simple manner to the Holy See, and may be further punished by the ordinary with privation of office or benefice.[75]

A chancellor who abuses the power of his office and betrays the trust confided in him with reference to the archives must be subjected to punishment. He is among the officials mentioned in canon 2406, § 1, who are bound by their office to prepare, write and preserve the documents or books of the curia, and who, if they presume to falsify, change, destroy or hide any of them, are to be punished by the ordinary either with deprivation of office or with other grave penalties in proportion to their guilt. They would not incur this punishment *ipso facto,* however, and before it could be imposed upon them it would be required that their crime be committed with full knowledge and deliberation. But if these elements are present, the ordinary must inflict a penalty.

Article 4. Use

Can. 378, § 1: Ex archivo non licet efferre scripturas sine Episcopi vel Vicarii Generalis consensu eaedemque post triduum in suum locum referantur. Ordinario autem reservatur facultas prorogandi hoc tempus, quae tamen prorogatio nonnisi moderate concedatur.

§ 2: Qui aliquam scripturam ex archivo effert, syngrapham sua manu signatam, hoc ipsum significantem, cancellario relinquat.

75. Canon 2405. Archbishop Rozman in "Cerkveno arhivno pravo"—*Bogoslovni Vestnik,* IV (1924), 155, states that this punishment applies only to clerics, since it appears in the Code under the title "De abusu potestatis vel officii ecclesiastici." But practically all other authors rightly include laymen under this penalty; e. g., Cappello, *Tractatus Canonico-Moralis De Censuris iuxta Codicem Iuris Canonici* (3. ed., Taurinorum Augustae: Marietti, 1933), p. 315; Cerato, *Censurae Vigentes Ipso Facto a Codice Iuris Canonici* (2. ed., Patavii: Typis Seminarii, 1921), p. 138; Cocchi, *Commentarium in Codicem Iuris Canonici ad usum scholarum,* Vol. VIII (4. ed., Taurinorum Augustae, Marietti, 1938), p. 400; Augustine, *A Commentary on Canon Law,* Vol. VII (3. ed., St. Louis: B. Herder & Co., 1931), 507. The last phrase of the canon, "et ab Ordinario etiam privatione officii, beneficii, plecti poterunt", cannot be urged against the latter opinion, because laymen also may hold ecclesiastical offices in a curia, e. g., that of notary (canon 373, § 3).

Can. 384, § 1: Documenta quae in . . . curiarum archivis sub secreto servanda non sunt, fit cuilibet cuius intersit inspiciendi potestas; itemque postulandi ut sua impensa sibi legitimum eorum exemplar exscribatur et tradatur.

§ 2: Cancellarii autem curiarum, . . . in communicandis documentis et eorum exemplaribus describendis tradendisque regulas servent a legitima auctoritate ecclesiastica datas, et in casibus dubiis loci Ordinarium consulant.

Although the use of diocesan archives is afforded to those who may have a legitimate interest in their contents, they are not intended to serve the general public. Their very purpose of preserving documents belonging to the Church, and of assisting the bishop in his administration, demands that their use be restricted. So the Code establishes definite rules to govern the removal of documents from the archives as well as their simple inspection.

A. *The Loaning of Documents*

More special are the precautions necessary when there is question of taking documents away, and canon 378 mentions the conditions under which this may be done. The canon states in the first place that it is unlawful to take writings out of the archives without the consent of the bishop or the vicar-general. In granting such a permission these ordinaries should use much discretion, considering the trustworthiness of the person seeking the favor, and the number, value or importance of the documents requested.[76] They should also inquire into the reason why a document is sought and take care that it will not be put to wrong uses.[77]

A permission to take documents from the archives need not be obtained from the chancellor, nor would it prove sufficient if perchance it were granted by him.[78] For although a license must be obtained

76. Cf. Rozman, "Cerkveno arhivno pravo", *Bogoslovni Vestnik,* IV (1924), 151.

77. Cf. Augustine, *A Commentary on the New Code of Canon Law,* II, 413.

78. Cf. Coronata, *Institutiones Iuris Canonici,* I, n. 428, 5°; Sipos, *Enchiridion Iuris Canonici,* p. 262.

from him to enter the archives, he has no authority whatever to allow documents to be removed. In fact, Blat so limits the chancellor's own use of the archives as to maintain that it is unlawful even for this official to take a document away without the bishop's consent.[79] Rozman disagrees with this opinion, claiming it to be contrary to the mind of the Code. He argues that since he to whom a document is given must hand over a receipt for it to the chancellor, as paragraph two of this canon provides, then the chancellor himself, if he were not allowed to take documents away from the archives, would be forced to give a receipt to himself, or to the bishop, which latter requirement, however, is not explicitly stated in the canon. He further urges that by choosing the chancellor as the guardian of the archives, the bishop has thereby given him all the rights belonging to that office from the common law.[80] But, while it may sound absurd to say that the chancellor must give himself a receipt, it must be admitted that he should place among the receipts some signed memorandum of his withdrawal of a document, if only for the sake of efficiency. Besides, even if the chancellor were excused from leaving a receipt, he would not necessarily be exempt from the obligation of obtaining the bishop's consent to take away a document, which is the point under discussion. And in no place does the Code attach to the position of chancellor the right to carry away a document from the archives without the permission of the ordinary. It would seem, then, that Blat's opinion must be upheld, at least in the sense that the ordinary's consent is necessary, not indeed each and every time the chancellor wishes to take out a document, but at least as a permission which the bishop at the time he appoints his chancellor grants him for all occasions until the permission shall be revoked.

It is certain also that during the vacancy of the see the vicar capitular or diocesan administrator has no power to permit the removal of documents from the archives, since he is himself forbidden to take them.[81]

Writings which have been taken out with the proper permission must be returned after three days. In determining this time the

79. *Commentarium Textus Codicis Iuris Canonici,* II, *De Personis,* n. 414.
80. "Cerkveno arhivno pravo", *Bogoslovni Vestnik,* IV (1924), 151 and 152.
81. Canon 435, § 3.

Code follows the provision of Benedict XIII's constitution[82] and holds a mean between extremes found in other earlier particular legislation.[83] The period of three days will be reckoned by beginning the computation from the very moment the document is handed over for its removal. Seventy-two hours later, that is, at the recurrence on the third succeeding day of the corresponding moment at which the document was removed, the return of the document must be an accomplished fact.[84] Only the bishop or the vicar-general may extend this time, but the canon warns him not to do so too freely. Therefore he should have a special reason for prolonging the permission,[85] and should not allow the documents to be kept out of the archives indefinitely. Some interpret the word "moderately" in the canon as implying that the prorogation should not be for more than another three days,[86] but the law itself sets no precise limitation. Consequently the ordinary may use his own prudence in the matter and fix the time for the documents' return according as circumstances may suggest or direct in the case.[87]

Despite all precautions on the part of the ordinary when lending a document, its safety is very uncertain after it has been taken away from the archives. Wisely then does the canon demand that a receipt for it be left with the chancellor by the person to whom it is given. This memorandum should indicate the date and hour when the document was taken away, furnish an adequate description of the document and bear the signature of the borrower. Rather than on loose slips of paper, these records will better be kept in a special book, as the

82. "*Maxima vigilantia,*" June 14, 1727, § 22 — *Bullarium Romanum,* XXII, 565; *Fontes,* n. 293.

83. E. g., the Council of Ravenna (1568) prohibited writings being taken out of diocesan archives under any condition whatsoever, while the Council of Mount Lebanon allowed the bishop to loan them for fifteen days. Cf. *supra,* Chapter III, Article 4, pp. 35-36.

84. Cf. canon 34, § 2, and Blat, *Commentarium Textus Codicis Iuris Canonici,* II, *De Personis,* n. 414.

85. Cf. Chelodi, *Ius De Personis,* n. 202.

86. Cf. Blat, *loc. cit.,* and Ayrinhac, *The Constitution of the Church in the New Code of Canon Law,* p. 219.

87. Cf. Toso, *Ad Codicem Iuris Canonici Commentaria Minora,* Lib. II, *De Personis,* Pars I, Tom. III, p. 23.

regulation of Benedict XIII suggested.[88] The obligation of demanding the receipt rests with the chancellor.[89] Because of the custody over the archives required of him by his office, it seems that he will also be responsible for the work of keeping track of the loaned documents and of reporting to the bishop those that have not been returned promptly.

B. *The Inspection of Documents*

The law recognizes the fact that occasions will arise when others besides the bishop may have to see documents contained in the archives, even if there is no necessity of taking them away. At times ecclesiastical officials, as, for example, judges and pastors, will have urgent need of inspecting them, and even private persons,[90] such as historians, may have a legitimate reason for wishing to refer to them. So, not wanting unreasonably to keep back any information which the documents may reveal, and still less wishing to impede with unnecessary inconvenience those who are carrying on the work of the Church, the Legislator grants certain permissions with regard to the examination of original documents and the obtaining of copies. Canon 384 states that writings which are not of a secret nature[91] may be examined by anyone whom they concern, and that such a person has also the right of asking for certified copies of documents, provided he will bear the expense which may be entailed in granting such inspection or in furnishing certified copies.

In providing documents for inspection or in making out or handing over copies, the chancellor is admonished to observe the rules of ecclesiastical superiors and in doubtful cases to consult the ordinary. The Code itself has enacted a law with regard to the issuing of copies, which law forbids the chancellor to give out copies of judicial acts and other documents pertaining to trials without a mandate from

88. Cf. const. "*Maxima vigilantia,*" June 14, 1727, § 22—*Bullarium Romanum,* XXII, 565; *Fontes,* n. 293.

89. Cf. Wernz-Vidal, *Ius Canonicum,* II, n. 647; Toso, *loc. cit.*

90. Cf. Rozman, "Cerkveno arhivno pravo", *Bogoslovni Vestnik,* IV (1924), 151.

91. The documents which must be preserved in the secret archives will be considered in a subsequent chapter.

the judge.[92] Every chancery, however, should have its own regulations. These could determine, for example, the precise place where documents may be examined; the precautions to be taken by the chancellor, such as his remaining present during the inspection or his guarding against the separation of documents which must be preserved together; the reasons for which and under what conditions copies may be obtained; the tax to be asked for such copies; and, in short, whatever else local circumstances may suggest for a proper compliance with the law of the canon.

At this point it seems opportune to recall the canonical penalty to which chancellors are liable who wilfully refuse to transmit or show acts, documents or books to anyone lawfully seeking them, or who in any other manner betray their trust. For such abuses they may be punished by the ordinary with privation or suspension from office and with the payment of any fines fixed by the ordinary in proportion to the gravity of the fault.[93]

92. Canon 1645, § 3.
93. Canon 2406, § 2.

CHAPTER V

SECRET DIOCESAN ARCHIVES

Some of the affairs pertaining to the administration of a diocese are of a secret character, either by their very nature or by a determination of the law. In attending to these duties the ordinary obtains documents which must be isolated from the other writings of the office and kept from the eyes of almost everyone, even of those who may have access to the common archives. Deep concern for such documents is shown by the Legislator when he gives to bishops detailed directions with regard to the erection, contents, use and custody of *secret* archives.

ARTICLE 1. ERECTION AND CONTENTS

A. *Erection*

> *Can. 379, § 1: "Habeant praeterea Episcopi aliud archivum secretum vel saltem in communi archivo armarium seu scrinium omnino clausum et obseratum, quod de loco amoveri nequeat...."*

The obligation of having secret archives is expressly imposed on all bishops. These archives may be established, if it be so desired, in a room separate from the general archives; but because in most dioceses a distinct room will be unnecessary due to the small number of documents, the law permits the secret archives to be set up in the same place as the common archives, and to be, within the latter, simply a closet or a case capable of preserving documents. The canon does insist, however, that the secret archives be entirely closed and locked, and that they be immovable. Rather than one of the ordinary filing cabinets, a wall-safe or a large, heavy safe would more appropriately meet these requirements,[1] provided it has two different locks as § 3 of the canon demands. This could be arranged by having a safe in which is built an inner door with the usual type of lock, and using

1. Cf. Augustine, *A Commentary on the New Code of Canon Law*, II, 415.

the combination lock on the outer door as the second one required. Within the archive could be placed compartments specially made, of number and size according to necessity. But no matter of what form the secret archive is, it should be located in a place at least equally as safe and suitable as is that of the common archives.

B. *Contents*

> *Can. 379, § 1: "...In eo scripturae secreto servandae cautissime custodiantur; sed singulis annis quamprimum comburantur documenta causarum criminalium in materia morum, quarum rei vita cesserint vel quae a decennio sententia condemnatoria absolutae sunt, retento facti brevi summario cum textu sententiae definitivae."*

The canon states that in the secret archives are to be most carefully guarded those writings which must be preserved secretly. Only one kind of document is expressly mentioned in this canon, namely, documents pertaining to criminal processes which deal with matters of morality. But elsewhere the Code explicitly commands that other writings be placed in the secret archives. Such are, for example, records of dispensations granted in the internal non-sacramental forum from occult impediments to marriage;[2] the special book containing notations of marriages of conscience and of the baptisms of children born from such marriages;[3] documents of a completed process, the nature of which demands secrecy;[4] the *acta* of an inquisition which precedes a criminal trial;[5] and the documents which prove that formal admonition or rebuke has been given to a party.[6] Implicitly demanded by the Code is the preservation in the secret archives of a book containing the records of dispensations conceded in the internal non-sacramental forum from irregularities or impediments to holy orders.[7]

2. Canon 1047.
3. Canon 1107.
4. Canon 1645, § 2.
5. Canon 1946, § 2, nn. 1 and 2.
6. Canon 2309, § 5.
7. Canon 991, § 4.

Many other confidential writings, such as those pertaining to the secret of the Holy Office[8] or to the life and morals of clerics, to suspension, removal from office,[9] or even the minutes of meetings held by the canons of the cathedral chapter or the diocesan consultors, although not referred to in the Code as material for the secret archives, may be regarded as being comprised in the generic phrase of the canon. It would seem that apart from the documents specified by the law, the determination of which documents or records are to be kept in the secret archives is left to the bishop.[10]

In order that the necessary secrecy with regard to criminal trials in moral matters may be the better preserved, the law demands that every year the contents of the secret archives be examined and as soon as possible after the death of a guilty party or after the lapse of ten years from the pronouncement of his condemnatory sentence, the documents of these processes be burned. There appears to be little need to stress the evident purpose or the seriousness of this law. By making it the Legislator reveals his desire that all such documents disappear in order so to protect the reputation of delinquents, that after many years, when memory of their crime is already erased from the minds of the people, no one will be able to obtain knowledge of the details of the case, not even the bishop to whom the secret archives are entrusted.[11] However, more important than this charitable consideration for the good name of individuals is the fact that timely destruction of the documents may prevent scandal and avoid unjust, unnecessary and embarrassing attacks upon the Church, by making it impossible for such documents to fall into the hands of her enemies. The law also has the practical value of preventing the useless accumulation of writings in the secret archives.[12]

8. Blat, *Commentarium Textus Codicis Iuris Canonici,* II, *De Personis,* n. 415.

9. Cf. canon 2144, § 1; Wernz-Vidal, *Ius Canonicum,* II, n. 648; Toso, *Ad Codicem Iuris Canonici Commentaria Minora,* Lib. II, *De Personis,* Pars I, Tom. III, p. 24.

10. Cf. Goyeneche, *Juris Canonici Summa Principia,* I, 324.

11. Cf. Rozman, "Cerkveno arhivno pravo", *Bogoslovni Vestnik,* IV (1924), 153; Augustine, *A Commentary on the New Code of Canon Law,* II, 415.

12. Cf. Augustine, *loc. cit.;* D'Angelo, *La Curia Diocesana,* p. 111.

The canon expressly states that the documents are to be destroyed by burning, therefore not merely by tearing them. The ten years after the condemnatory sentence are to be computed according to canon 34, § 3, nn. 1 and 3;[13] but if no such sentence was passed the rule for burning the documents does not apply.[14] Even in the latter case, however, there will ordinarily be no reason for preserving any longer the documents of this nature[15] and the purpose of the law suggests that they also be destroyed.

Although the documents must be burned, some record of the criminal processes must be retained. Perhaps to protect the Church against future legal action, which may possibly be brought by one of the guilty persons or his relatives, the law wishes that there be preserved a brief summary of the facts of the case and the text of the final sentence. This record, of course, should remain in the secret archives after the documents are destroyed.

No mention is made in the canon of any arrangement for the writings in the secret archives, but it is obvious that they should be disposed in some orderly manner, which the bishop may decide. Perhaps the easiest arrangement, since the documents are usually so few, would be an alphabetical one determined by the names of the parties with whom the writings are concerned. The documents pertaining to each person could be placed chronologically in a separate folder and the folder inscribed with the name of the person. It may also prove appropriate to separate the documents pertaining to the diocesan tribunal from the others, and to assign to each group a distinct space in the archive. If the number of documents makes it necessary, the folders could again be divided according to the years to which they belong, in which case the face of each compartment in the archives should be marked in some manner to indicate not only the classification of the documents but the year or period of years to which they refer, as, for example, Criminal Processes, 1935-1940, or Marriages of Conscience, 1930-1940, etc.

13. Cf. Blat, *Commentarium Textus Codicis Iuris Canonici*, II, *De Personis*, n. 415.

14. Cf. Ayrinhac, *Constitution of the Church in the New Code of Canon Law*, p. 219.

15. Cf. cc. 1702 and 1703 regarding the *tempus utile* for instituting criminal processes.

Article 2. Custody

The very reason for secret archives as well as the wording of this first canon pertaining to them[16] intimates the special precautions that will be necessary to preserve the secrecy of their writings. It is not surprising, then, that most of the laws enacted regarding secret archives deal with their custody, either when the bishop is actually ruling his diocese or when the see is impeded or vacant.

Before considering these laws, however, it seems that an explanation should be given of the reason why the Apostolic Administrator is especially mentioned in these and the subsequent canons which treat of the use of secret archives. Augustine suggests that it is because this official has sometimes been excluded not only from the episcopal palace but also from the diocesan archives.[17] But a better reason could be deduced from the canonical distinction that is made between a permanent and a temporary Apostolic Administrator. According to canon 315, § 1, an Apostolic Administrator who is constituted for a diocese permanently enjoys *the same rights as a residential bishop,* while § 2, n. 1, of the same canon states that one given only temporarily has *the rights of a vicar capitular,* but that if the bishop is still in possession of his see the Apostolic Administrator may hold the canonical visitation of the diocese. In the canons dealing with secret archives no such distinction is made by the Legislator and apparently his avoidance of it is intentional. For if the rights with reference to secret archives which these canons confer were meant only for the permanent Apostolic Administrator, every mention of that official would be superfluous, since the permanent Apostolic Administrator would already have these rights, along with all the other rights of a bishop. So it would seem that in this place the law, by directly alluding to the Apostolic Administrator without distinction, wishes it to be understood that the *temporary* Apostolic Administrator also is being given the same rights in this matter as a residential bishop; and that he will have, therefore, other rights over and above those of a vicar capitular, namely, of inspecting the documents of the secret archives alone and

16. "... In eo scripturae secreto servandae *cautissime* custodiantur."

17. *A Commentary on the New Code of Canon Law,* II, 415.

without witnesses, of having these archives remain unsealed while he is ruling the diocese, etc.

A. *Custody When the See Is Occupied*

> *Can. 379, § 2: Etiam huius secreti archivi vel armarii inventarium seu catalogus conficiatur ad normam can. 375, § 2.*
>
> *§ 3. Hoc archivum vel armarium duabus clavibus inter se diversis aperiatur, quarum altera apud Episcopum vel Administratorem Apostolicum, altera apud Vicarium Generalem vel, eo deficiente, Curiae cancellarium asservetur.*

Just as for the general archives, so also for the secret, an inventory or catalogue of the documents must be compiled, giving a brief summary of each writing. Evidently this is for the same purpose as the inventory of the general archives, namely, to afford the bishop a means of knowing what documents belong in the secret archives and thereby to help him guard them more carefully. Any form of inventory may be used, and perhaps for this smaller archive the bound book will be the most convenient.[18] If this is used, it will be necessary merely to list the documents pertaining to each person on a separate page, and to have an alphabetical index of the names in the front or back of the book, with the number of the page written opposite the corresponding name of the person. This inventory should be diligently and *secretly* guarded.[19]

The Code does not say by whom the inventory is to be made. It seems that the chancellor may do it, provided that an oath of secrecy is taken by him.[20]

It is to be noted that while the law refers back to canon 375, § 2, which commands the making of an inventory for the common archives, it does not require, as is demanded by canon 376, § 1 for the general archives, that the inventory be examined every year to keep it up to date. Rightly is this latter reference omitted, for the inventory of the

18. Cf. *supra,* Chap. IV, Art. 3, p. 57.

19. Cf. Rozman, "Cerkveno arhivno pravo", *Bogoslovni Vestnik,* IV (1924), 152.

20. Cf. Coronata, *Institutiones Iuris Canonici,* I, n. 429, 3°, a, footnote 7; Goyeneche, *Juris Canonici Summa Principia,* I, 325, footnote 9.

secret archives will not need the same frequent and habitual attention as that of the larger archives.[21] However, this does not mean that the inventory of the secret archives may be neglected. It would be very simple as well as most practical to complete it gradually as often as a new document is placed in the archives.

The secret archives must be locked with two keys, so unlike each other that two different locks are required. One of these keys is to be retained by the bishop or the Apostolic Administrator. The latter is mentioned because when he is placed in charge of a diocese *sede plena,* the jurisdiction of the bishop is suspended,[22] and the Apostolic Administrator assumes among the other episcopal rights the control of the archives. The other key is to be kept by the vicar-general, or, if the office of vicar-general is vacant or if that official is absent, by the chancellor. Obviously the phrase *eo deficiente* in the canon points to the case in which there happens to be no vicar-general holding office, as Rozman[23] and Ayrinhac[24] state. But as Blat interprets it, it may also refer to the circumstance in which, although there is a vicar-general in office, he is not actually present;[25] for if he were still to retain the key during a prolonged absence from the office, the bishop's right to use the archives would be greatly restricted.[26]

Should a diocese have more than one vicar-general, the bishop may designate the one who is to have charge of the key, but in all likelihood the convenience of the bishop will be best served if the key is in the possession of the vicar-general who resides nearest the office or who frequents it most. Since Vicariates and Prefectures Apostolic have no vicar-general, the second key could be held by the provicar or the pro-prefect.[27]

The very provision of this law which requires the two keys and the intervention of two different persons for opening the archives is an

21. Cf. Blat, *Commentarium Textus Codicis Iuris Canonici,* II, *De Personis,* n. 415.

22. Canon 316, § 1.

23. "Cerkveno arhivno pravo", *Bogoslovni Vestnik,* IV (1924), 152.

24. *Constitution of the Church in the New Code of Canon Law,* p. 220.

25. *Commentarium Textus Codicis Iuris Canonici,* II, *De Personis,* n. 415.

26. Cf. canon 379, § 4.

27. Canon 309, § 2. Cf. Coronata, *Institutiones Iuris Canonici,* I, n. 429, 3°, c, footnote.

indication of the extraordinary care with which the keys must be guarded by those to whom they are entrusted. The place where they are reserved by the vicar-general or the chancellor should be secret, but known to the bishop.[28]

B. *Custody When the See Is Impeded or Vacant*

In the course of its history a diocese will at certain times be without the rule of its own bishop. On the one hand, it may happen that, although the episcopal see has an incumbent who still retains office, the bishop is unable to discharge the functions of his office because of some obstacle; on the other hand, the diocese actually may not have a lawfully constituted bishop. The Code refers to these periods respectively as intervals when the see is impeded or vacant, enumerates the causes which may bring them about, and determines upon whom the rule of the diocese will devolve in each event.[29] It is during times such as these that the custody of the secret archives more readily suffers neglect.[30] Realizing this, the Legislator by certain enactments has carefully devised a system for safeguarding the secret writings during those intervals when the government of the diocese is not provided for in a *special* way by the Holy See.[31] The enactments regulate the custody of the keys and the sealing of the secret archives.

1) *Custody of the Keys*

Can. 380: Statim a capta possessione, Episcopus sacerdotem designet, qui, sede vacante aut impedita, clavem secreti tabularii seu armarii quae apud Episcopum erat, assumat.

28. The question as to how these keys are to be used will be considered in a subsequent article within this chapter.

29. Cf. cc. 429; 430, § 1; 431, § 1; 432, § 1.

30. Cf. Toso, *Ad Codicem Iuris Canonici Commenteria Minoria,* Lib. II, *De Personis,* Pars I, Tom. III, p. 24.

31. These rules do not apply, for example, if an Apostolic Administrator is ruling the diocese at the time when the see becomes vacant (cf. Coronata, *Institutiones Iuris Canonici,* I, n. 429, 3°, f) or impeded, for the bishop's key to the secret archives which is already in the Apostolic Administrator's possession according to canon 379, § 3, will be retained by him. Cf. Blat, *Commentarium Textus Codicis Iuris Canonici,* II, *De Personis,* n. 417.

> *Can. 381, § 1: Nisi Administrator Apostolicus dioecesi datus fuerit:*
> *1° Sede impedita ad normam can. 429, § 1, sacerdos ab Episcopo designatus, si quidem regimen dioecesis sit penes virum ecclesiasticum ab Episcopo delegatum, clavem eidem remittat; si penes Vicarium Generalem, eam ipse retineat;*
> *2° Sede vero vacante aut impedita ad normam cit. can. 429, § 3, idem sacerdos clavem remittat Vicario Capitulari statim post eius designationem; Vicarius vero Generalis vel cancellarius aliam clavem a se retentam remittere eodem tempore debet primae Capituli dignitati vel consultori dioecesano munere antiquiori.*

A provision is made which imposes an obligation on the bishop himself when he first begins to rule over his diocese. It is intended to forestall appropriation by the wrong parties of the bishop's own key to the secret archives when he may no longer be able to take care of it. Canon 380 states that immediately after he has taken possession of his diocese the bishop must designate a priest who will assume custody of his key whenever the see becomes vacant or impeded.[32] Any priest of the diocese, whether he is a member of the curia or not, may be selected for this trust. It is recommended that the designation of the priest be made in writing and in two copies, one to remain in the common archives and the other to be given to the priest himself, in order that he may be able to prove his appointment whenever proof may be required.[33] It is manifest that the bishop should inform the priest of the location of the key and the manner in which he may easily be able to obtain it.

As soon as possible after he has learned that the see is impeded or vacant the priest should take possession of the bishop's key and retain it until such time as he delivers it to the ecclesiastic upon whom will devolve the administration of the diocese. His rôle, therefore, is simply that of a fiduciary and he has no right to enter the secret

32. Because a permanent Apostolic Administrator is held to the same obligations as a bishop, he also should appoint a priest for this purpose. Cf. Coronata, *op. cit.*, n. 429, 3°, e, footnote.

33. Cf. D'Angelo, *La Curia Diocesana*, p. 111, footnote 5.

archives alone.[34] The following contingencies determine when and to whom the priest will surrender the key.

a) According to canon 429, § 1, if the see becomes impeded due to the bishop's captivity, banishment,[35] exile[36] or disability, so that he cannot communicate with his diocese even by letters,[37] the administration is to be assumed by the vicar-general if he is present and not impeded, or by another ecclesiastic whom the bishop may have delegated.[38] If the vicar-general takes up the rule, since he already has the second key to the archives, the priest will keep the bishop's key; because all these precautions are for the purpose of preventing both keys coming into the hands of one person.[39] If another ecclesiastic delegated by the bishop is to administer the diocese, the priest gives the bishop's key to him.

b) If the see becomes impeded for the same reasons but the vicar-general is absent or impeded and no other ecclesiastic has been delegated by the bishop as administrator, the cathedral chapter (or diocesan consultors)[40] must elect one of their members who will govern the diocese with the powers of a vicar capitular (diocesan administrator). In this event the priest will hand over the bishop's key to the vicar capitular (diocesan administrator) immediately after his election.

c) If the see becomes vacant then the vicar capitular (diocesan administrator) receives the bishop's key upon his election by the cathedral chapter (diocesan consultors) to rule the diocese during its vacancy.[41]

It remains now to investigate what disposition is to be made of the second key to the secret archives. In the meanwhile it has been in the possession of the vicar-general or of the chancellor. The canon states that when the vicar capitular is to assume the rule of a vacant or an

34. Rozman, "Cerkveno arhivno pravo", *Bogoslovni Vestnik,* IV (1924), 153.

35. Compulsion to live in a certain place. Cf. canon 2298, 8°.

36. Expulsion from one's country; but cf. canon 2298, 7°.

37. Goyeneche evidently misread the canon, for he writes, "ita ut Episcopus *possit* ipsam gubernare per litteras". — *Juris Canonici Summa Principia.,* I, p. 325, n. 4.

38. Cf. canon 366, § 3.

39. Cf. Chelodi, *Ius De Personis,* n. 202.

40. Cf. canon 427.

41. Cf. canon 432, §§ 1 and 2.

impeded diocese in the two cases described above in b) and c), the other key must be given to the first dignitary of the cathedral chapter or to the oldest diocesan consultor[42] at the same time that the bishop's key is being surrendered by the priest fiduciary to the vicar capitular.

2) *Sealing of the Archives*

Can. 381, § 2: Antequam claves iis, quibus tradi debent ad normam § 1, remissae fuerint, Vicarius Generalis vel cancellarius et sacerdos, ut supra, ab Episcopo designatus, tabularium vel armarium sigillis Curiae obsignent.

Before the keys to the secret archives change hands in the abovementioned circumstances, the vicar-general (chancellor) and the priest holding the bishop's key must close up the secret archives with the seals of the curia. This provision apparently means that wire and lead, sealing wax or some other substance, stamped with the impression of the diocesan seals, must be so affixed to the door of the archives that the door cannot be opened without breaking the seal. The purpose is to inform the impeded bishop on his return, or the newly appointed bishop on his arrival, of any possible actions committed contrary to the prohibition stated in the following canon, which prohibition forbids opening of the archives during the time when the see is vacant or impeded.

Whether or not the archives must be sealed in all the cases described above is not definitely clear from the words of the legislation. The canon states that this must be done before the keys are handed over to those who should receive them *according to* § *1;* and it makes no distinction between numbers 1 and 2 of the paragraph, which together provide for all three contingencies. But Blat,[43] Prümmer[44] and D'An-

42. If he who holds the highest dignity in the chapter or who is the oldest diocesan consultor has been chosen vicar capitular or diocesan administrator, then, since both keys should not be in the hands of the same person, this key should be given to the second dignitary in rank or to the second oldest consultor. Cf. Wernz-Vidal, *Ius Canonicum,* II, n. 648, footnote 42.

43. *Commentarium Textus Codicis Iuris Canonici,* II, *De Personis,* n. 417, 2°.

44. *Manuale Iuris Canonici,* Q. 134, 2.

gelo[45] hold that the sealing must be done only when the vicar capitular is to assume the rule of the diocese. Blat points out that when the ecclesiastic delegated by the bishop is to rule the diocese only *one* key is transferred; and when the vicar-general is to become administrator, *neither* key is turned over to anyone. He concludes that, since it is only when the vicar capitular is to administer the diocese that *keys* (in the plural) are handed over, it is then only that the law applies. However, the plural number "keys" would have to be used also if the word were intended to refer to all three cases. Besides, it is undoubtedly the mind of the Legislator to provide for this special protection of sealing the secret archives whenever the see is impeded or vacant, without reference to the person upon whom the administration of the diocese devolves in the circumstances under consideration. Certainly the same dangers to the archives could be present just as much under one temporary administrator as under another.[46] Therefore, until an authoritative interpretation of the law on this point will have definitely sanctioned the alleged distinction between § 1, n. 1 and § 1, n. 2 of the canon, the distinction should not be made. On the contrary, the obligation of the vicar-general and of the priest who has assumed the bishop's key to seal the archives would seem to apply in every case referred to in the canon.

ARTICLE 3. USE

It will be recalled that the permission to inspect the documents contained in the common archives when granted to anyone to whom the documents are of legitimate concern explicitly excludes the examination of documents which must be *secretly* preserved.[47] This is to be expected, for the nature of the secret documents requires that their use be much more limited. Particularly is this true when there is no bishop present in the diocese to guard the secrecy of the documents. The Code therefore lays down definite rules for the use of the secret archives both when the bishop is present and when the see is vacant or impeded.

45. *La Curia Diocesana,* p. 112, footnote 3.
46. Cf. canon 18.
47. Canon 384, § 1.

A. *Use When the See Is Occupied*

Can. 379, § 4: Episcopus vel Administrator Apostolicus, repetita altera clave, ipse solus, nemine adstante, archivum vel armarium secretum, ubi opus fuerit, aperire et inspicere potest, quod deinde utraque clavi iterum claudatur.

The right to use the secret archives is reserved by law to the bishop when he is actually ruling his diocese. Canon 379, § 4, states that the bishop or Apostolic Administrator may open and inspect the archives without any witnesses. With regard to the manner in which this right may be exercised the canon explains that the bishop or Apostolic Administrator may demand the other key to the secret archives from the vicar-general or the chancellor. From this it is quite clear that the purpose of the two keys is not to restrict in any way the liberty of the bishop, but simply by means of this added precaution to make it more difficult for anyone unlawfully to use the secret archives. Since, for using the archives, the bishop is expressly allowed by law to have both keys, the vicar-general or chancellor cannot refuse to surrender the one which is in his possession. His duty is a mere custody of the key and grants no authority respecting the archives themselves.

The only restrictions placed on the bishop in this matter are the conditions that there be a necessity for opening and using the archives and that when he has finished he relock the door. The necessity may be any legitimate one determined by the bishop himself. It is to be understood from § 3 of this same canon that, after using the archives and again fastening the lock, the bishop should return the other key to the vicar-general or the chancellor as soon as possible.[48]

It may be asked if persons other than the bishop or Apostolic Administrator may under any circumstances open the archives and examine the secret documents. There seems to be no reason for giving a negative reply if the archives are opened and the documents are then examined by the person *in the presence of witnesses;* for the law, by conceding to the bishop the right of opening the archives and examining the documents when he is alone certainly does not prohibit others from doing so if witnesses are present. Moreover, in order to open the

48. Cf. Blat, *Commentarium Textus Codicis Iuris Canonici,* II, *De Personis,* n. 415.

archives one would have to obtain the keys from the bishop and the vicar-general, which fact would give to these ordinaries the opportunity of ascertaining the circumstances of the person, his purpose for seeking the keys, etc.; and the presence of the witnesses would prevent resultant abuses if the keys were handed over.

But it can also be said rightly that others besides the bishop or the Apostolic Administrator may receive permission to open the archives and to inspect the documents *alone,* i. e., without witnesses. Rozman states that the use of the secret archives is allowed only to the bishop whenever necessity demands,[49] and D'Angelo remarks that it cannot be maintained that the vicar-general or the chancellor may open the archives and inspect the documents by himself.[50] Both of these statements are correct if they are intended in the sense that no person other than the bishop or Apostolic Administrator has *the right by law* to perform such actions. However, if the authors mean that the canor takes away from the bishop the faculty of permitting, for a just reason, the opening and inspection by other persons, even without witnesses, their opinion cannot be upheld.[51]

No mention is made in the canon of the question concerning the taking away of documents from the secret archives. Sipos[52] and Prümmer[53] assert inaccurately that this is never lawful.[54] It is true that when the see is vacant the vicar capitular is expressly forbidden to take away documents;[55] but since in this canon the Code states no such prohibition with reference to the bishop's use of the secret archives, it would seem that the taking away of documents is permitted to the bishop and to all other ordinaries equal to a bishop.[56]

49. Cf. "Cerkveno arhivno pravo", *Bogoslovni Vestnik,* IV (1924), 152.

50. Cf. *La Curia Diocesana,* p. 111, footnote 4.

51. Cf. Goyeneche, *Juris Canonici Summa Principia,* I, 325, footnote 11; Coronata, *Institutiones Iuris Canonici,* I, n. 429, 3, d, footnote.

52. *Enchiridion Iuris Canonici,* p. 263.

53. *Manuale Iuris Canonici,* Q. 134, 4.

54. The Code, at least in one instance, expressly provides for the removal of documents from the secret archives; cf. canon 1946, § 1, 1°, 2°, together with canon 1954.

55. Canon 382.

56. Cf. Coronata, *Institutiones Iuris Canonici,* I, n. 429, 3°, footnote; Goyeneche, *Juris Canonici Summa Principia,* I, 326, footnote 14.

B. *Use When the See Is Impeded or Vacant*

> *Can. 382, § 1: Tabularium vel armarium nunquam aperiatur nec sigilla ab eo removeantur, nisi urgente necessitate et ab ipso Vicario Capitulari coram duobus canonicis vel dioecesanis consultoribus, qui evigilent ne qua scriptura e tabulario auferatur; solus autem Vicarius Capitularis documenta in tabulario asservata potest, iisdem canonicis vel consultoribus adstantibus, inspicere, nunquam tamen auferre. Archivum autem, post inspectionem iterum sigillis obsignetur.*
>
> *§ 2: Advenienti novo Episcopo, si sigilla remota fuerint et tabularium aut armarium apertum, Vicarius Capitularis rationem reddat urgentis necessitatis, qua ad hoc motus fuerit.*

The last enactment of the Legislator is a provision for the use of secret diocesan archives when the see is impeded or vacant. Through this law the use of the archives during that time is denied almost to everyone. Except for one occasion the archives may never be opened nor the seals removed. Two distinct acts come under the prohibition, the opening of the archives and the removal of the seals, so that even if the archives are not intended to be opened, still the seals cannot be removed.

In order that the exception be valid three conditions are stated. The first demands that there be an urgent necessity. It is difficult to conceive an urgent necessity for the removal of the seals without any intention of opening the archives, unless it might be to affix the seals more securely if they had been originally attached in an improper manner. But the need for opening the archives could arise, for example, to inscribe in their proper books records recently received concerning a marriage of conscience or a dispensation granted in the internal non-sacramental forum, or to study the acts of a current criminal process which are already in the archives.[57] The second condition requires that the removal of the seals or the opening of the archives be done by the vicar capitular. No such exception is made, there-

57. Cf. Rozman, "Cerkveno arhivno pravo", *Bogoslovni Vestnik*, IV (1924), 153.

fore, for the vicar-general or for a priest delegated by the bishop if either should be administering the diocese when it is impeded. Coronata gives as an explanation for this omission the fact that the vicar-general or delegated priest could have been delegated beforehand by the bishop to remove the seals and open the archives, and would then have the same permission as when the bishop is present.[58] But the explicit wording of this provision made for an extraordinary circumstance[59] would invalidate any delegation of this kind, and the better opinion seems to be that of Ayrinhac, who holds that the vicar-general or priest delegated by the bishop to administer an impeded diocese may under no circumstances open the secret archives.[60] Because of the same clear statement of the canon it is also manifest that the vicar capitular cannot give permission to others to remove the seals or to open the archives.

The third condition that must be fulfilled before the removal of the seals or the opening of the archives is that these actions be done by the vicar capitular in the presence of two canons or by the diocesan administrator in the presence of two diocesan consultors. Consequently, the vicar capitular or diocesan administrator may never act alone in this matter. Which canons or diocesan consultors are to be selected is not specified, so the vicar capitular or diocesan administrator may choose any two whom he wishes.[61] As the canon states, their only obligation is to watch that no documents are taken away. They are given no right with regard to the examination of the documents in the secret archives.

This right by law is granted only to the vicar capitular or the diocesan administrator, who may inspect the documents while still in the presence of the two canons or consultors. With similar precautions, however, the vicar capitular or diocesan administrator may permit others to examine them; for he has the ordinary jurisdiction of a bishop in all spiritual and temporal affairs except in those which are

58. Cf. *Institutiones Iuris Canonici,* I, n. 429, 3°.

59. "Tabularium . . . *nunquam* aperiatur nec sigilla ab eo removeantur, *nisi. . . . ab ipso Vicario Capitulari. . . .*"

60. *Constitution of the Church in the New Code of Canon Law,* pp. 221-222.

61. Blat, *Commentarium Textus Codicis Iuris Canonici,* II, *De Personis,* n. 418.

expressly prohibited to him by law,[62] and the Code does not expressly forbid him to grant this permission.[63] But at no time nor for any reason may the vicar capitular or the diocesan administrator take documents away from the archives. When the necessity has been satisfied the archives must again be locked and sealed, whether with the same seals or others does not matter.[64]

If the seals were removed or the archives opened as described above, the vicar capitular or diocesan administrator is obliged to report to the new bishop the reason which urged him to do so. The canon mentions nothing of a similar report being made to an impeded bishop on his return to the diocese, but it seems that the law would apply also in this event. An Apostolic Administrator would not be subject to this enactment because he is held responsible only to the Holy See. Obviously, if the cause for opening the archives was not a just or sufficient one, or if abuses of any nature are discovered, the new or impeded bishop may take measures against the persons who were at fault.[65]

62. Canon 435, § 1.
63. Cf. Coronata, *Institutiones Iuris Canonici,* I, n. 429, 3°, γ, footnote 3.
64. Blat, *loc. cit.*
65. Cf. canon 444, § 1.

CONCLUSIONS

1. Diocesan archives are of ancient origin and were in use quite continuously and universally throughout the Church's history.

2. During the first sixteen centuries no precise laws existed regulating the maintenance of diocesan archives.

3. Because of the neglect of diocesan archives and the consequent abuses connected with their custody, definite legislation appeared between the sixteenth century and the publication of the Code.

4. Before the publication of the Code there were no universal laws of the Church dealing with diocesan archives. The laws that were enacted up to that time were in the nature of particular constitutions of Roman Pontiffs, of decrees of provincial councils, of statutes of diocesan synods, and of decrees or responses of the Sacred Congregations for specific localities.

5. The most outstanding and influential particular enactments regarding diocesan archives are contained in the constitution "*Maxima vigilantia,*" issued by Pope Benedict XIII on June 14, 1727. From this document many provisions were adopted substantially, and in some cases verbatim, in the present general laws concerning diocesan archives.

6. The canons of the Code, just as the earlier particular laws, lay directly on the bishop the final responsibility for the maintenance and custody of diocesan archives. However, by making this the principal duty of the chancellor, the present law also holds him accountable to a great extent.

7. Because of the purpose of diocesan archives the obligation of the bishop to establish and carefully guard them is a grave one.

8. Although the purpose of diocesan archives as especially emphasized by the Code is the *preservation* of the documents and writings belonging to the Church, if the archives are scientifically and faithfully maintained they may also serve the bishop by contributing to a more efficient administration of his diocese.

9. With comparatively few exceptions it is left to the bishop to determine which documents are to be preserved or destroyed and what method is to be used in arranging them in the archives.

10. Undoubtedly prompted by sad experiences of the Church during her history, the Legislator has enacted laws concerning the custody and use of secret archives which are very strict and detailed. This fact indicates the seriousness with which these laws should be regarded and the fidelity with which they should be observed.

BIBLIOGRAPHY

Sources

Acta Sanctae Sedis, 41 vols., Romae, 1865-1908.

Acta et Decreta Concilii Plenarii Americae Latinae in Urbe Celebrati, A. D. MDCCCXCIX, Romae, 1902.

Acta et Decreta Concilii Plenarii Australasiae habiti apud Sydney, 1885, Sydney, 1887.

Acta et Decreta Concilii Plenarii Baltimorensis Tertii, A. D. MDCCCLXXXIV, Baltimorae: John Murphy, 1886.

Acta et Decreta Concilii Provincialis Neo-Eboracensis Quarti, MDCCCLXXXIII, Neo-Eboraci, 1886.

Acta et Decreta Sacrorum Conciliorum Recentiorum, Collectio Lacensis, 7 vols., Friburgi Brisgoviae, 1870-1890.

Bullarium Diplomatum et Privilegiorum Sanctorum Romanorum Pontificum, Taurinensis Editio, 25 vols., Augustae Taurinorum, 1857-1872.

Codex Iuris Canonici, Pii X Pontificis Maximi iussu digestus, Benedicti Papae XV auctoritate promulgatus, Romae: Typis Polyglottis Vaticanis, 1917.

Codicis Iuris Canonici Fontes cura Emi. Petri Card. Gasparri editi, 9 vols., Romae (later Civitate Vaticana): Typis Polyglottis Vaticanis, 1923-1939 (Vols. VII, VIII, IX, ed. *cura et studio Emi. Justiniani Card. Serédi*).

Concilium Romanum in Sacrosancta Lateranensi Basilica Celebratum, Anno Universalis Jubilaei, MDCCXXV, Bruxellis, 1726.

Corpus Iuris Civilis, Vol. I, *Institutiones* — recognovit P. Krueger; *Digesta* — recognovit Theodorum Mommson, retractavit P. Krueger; Vol. II, *Codex Justinianus* — recognovit et retractavit P. Krueger; Vol. III, *Novellae Constitutiones* — R. Schoell; opus Schoell morte interceptum absolvit G. Kroll, Berolini, 1928-1929.

Harduin, Jean, *Acta Conciliorum et Epistolae Decretales ac Constitutiones Summorum Pontificum*, 12 vols., Parisiis, 1715.

Lucanae Ecclesiae Synodus Dioecesana, Lucae, 1887.

Mansi, Joannes, *Sacrorum Conciliorum Nova et Amplissima Collectio*, 53 vols., Parisiis, 1901-1927.

Monumenta Germaniae Historica, Legum Sectio, Capitularia Spuria, Tom. II, Pars II, ed. G. H. Pertz, Hannoverae, 1887.

Monumenta Germaniae Historica, Legum Sectio III, Concilia Aevi Karolini, Tom. II, Pars II, ed. A. Werminghoff, Hannoverae et Lipsiae, 1906.

Monumenta Germaniae Historica, Legum Sectio III, Concilia Aevi Merovingici, Tom. I, ed. Fredericus Maassen, Hannoverae, 1893.

Pallottini, Salvator, *Collectio Omnium Conclusionum et Resolutionum Quae in causis propositis apud Sacram Congregationem Cardinalium S. Concilii Tridentini Interpretum Prodierunt ab ejus institutione anno MDLXIV ad annum MDCCCLX, distinctis titulis alphabetico ordine per materias digesta*, 17 vols., Romae, 1868-1893.

Quaranta, Stephano, *Summa Bullarii Earumve Summorum Pontificum Constitutionum,* Venetiis, 1622.

Synodus Dioecesana Ferrariensis, MDCCLXXXI, Ferrariae, 1781.

AUTHORS

Ayrinhac, H. A., and Lydon, P. J., *Constitution of the Church in the New Code of Canon Law,* New York: Blase Benziger & Co., 1925.

[Bachofen], Charles Augustine, *A Commentary on Canon Law,* 8 vols., Vol. II, 5. ed., St. Louis: Herder, 1928; Vol. III, 3. ed., St. Louis: Herder, 1931.

Baronius, Caesar, S. R. E. Card., *Annales Ecclesiastici,* Tomus II, Barri-Ducis, 1864.

Benoist, E., *Oeuvres de Virgile,* Texte Latin, Paris, 1876.

Blat, Albertus, *Commentarium Textus Codicis Iuris Canonici,* 6 vols., Romae, 1921-1927; Liber II, *De Personis,* 2. ed., Romae: Del Collegio "Angelico", 1921.

Catholic Encyclopedia, The, 16 vols. and 2 suppls., New York, 1907-1922.

Cappello, Felice M., *Summa Iuris Canonici in usum scholarum concinnata,* Vol. I, 2. ed., Romae: Apud Aedes Universitatis Gregorianae, 1932.

———, *Tractatus Canonico-Moralis De Censuris iuxta Codicem Iuris Canonici,* 3. ed., Taurinorum Augustae: Marietti, 1933.

Cerato, Prodocimus, *Censurae Vigentes Ipso Facto a Codice Iuris Canonici,* 2. ed., Patavii: Typis Seminarii, 1921.

Chelodi, Joannes, *Ius de Personis iuxta Codicem Iuris Canonici,* 2. ed., Tridentini, 1927.

Cicognani, Amleto, *Canon Law,* authorized version by J. O'Hara and F. Brennan, Philadelphia: Dolphin Press, 1934.

Clark, Albertus C., *M. Tullii Ciceronis Orationes,* Oxonii, 1910.

Cocchi, Guidus, *Commentarium in Codicem Iuris Canonici ad usum scholarum,* Vol. VIII, 4. ed., Taurinorum Augustae: Marietti, 1938.

Coronata, Matthaeus Conte a, *Institutiones Iuris Canonici,* editio altera aucta et emendata, Vol. I, Taurini (Italia): Marietti, 1939.

C. Plini Secundi, Naturalis Historiae Libri XXXVII, ex Editione Gabrielis Brotier, 14 vols., Londini, 1826.

D'Angelo, Sosio, *La Curia Diocesana, a norma del Codice di Diritto Canonico,* Giarre (Sicilia): Pietro Lisi, 1922.

De Meester, Alphonsus, *Juris Canonici et Juris Canonico-Civilis Compendium,* Vol. II, Brugis: Desclée, De Brouwer et Si, 1923.

Dictionnaire Raisonné de Diplomatique Chrétienne, Paris, 1846.

DuCange, Carolus Dufresne, *Glossarium ad Scriptores Mediae et Infimae Latinitatis,* 6 vols., Parisiis, 1733.

Enciclopedia Italiana, ed. Giovanni Treccani, Milano, 1929-1939.

Encyclopédie des Gens du Monde, 22 vols., Paris, 1833-1844.

Ferraris, F. Lucius, *Prompta Bibliotheca, Canonica, Juridica, Moralis, Theologica, nec non Ascetica, Polemica, Rubricistica, Historica,* 9 vols., Romae, 1885-1899.

Forcellini, A., Facciolati, J., *Lexicon Totius Latinitatis,* 5 vols., Patavii, 1871.

Goyeneche, S., *Juris Canonici Summa Principia,* Romae: Tip. Pol. "Cuore di Maria", pro manuscripto, I, 1935.

Jenkinson, Hilary, *A Manual of Archive Administration,* 2. ed., London: Percy Lund, Humphrey & Co., Ltd., 1937.

Lucidi, Angelus, *De Visitatione Sacrorum Liminum,* 3. ed., 3 vols., Romae, 1883.

Migne, Jacques Paul, *Encyclopédie Théologique;* Tom. 26, *Dictionnaire de Discipline Ecclésiastique,* 2 vols., Paris, 1856.

———, *Patrologiae Cursus Completus, Series Latina,* 221 vols., Paris, 1844-1864.

O'Rourke, James J., *Parish Registers,* The Catholic University of America, Canon Law Studies, n. 88, Washington, D. C.: The Catholic University of America Press, 1934.

Pignatelli, Jacobus, *Consultationes Canonicae,* 11 vols. in 4, Coloniae Allobrogum, 1700.

Prümmer, Dominicus, *Manuale Iuris Canonici,* 3. ed., Friburgi Brisgoviae: Herder & Co., 1922.

Schneider, Philipp, *Die Entwicklung der bischoeflichen Dom Kapitel bis zum vierzehnter Jahrhundert,* Mainz, 1882.

Sipos, Stephanus, *Enchiridion Iuris Canonici,* Pecs: Haladus, R. T., 1926.

Thomassinus, Ludovicus, *Vetus et Nova Ecclesiae Disciplina Circa Beneficia et Beneficiarios,* 3 vols., Magontiaci, 1787.

Toso, Albertus, *Ad Codicem Iuris Canonici Benedicti XV Pontificis Maximi,* Ephemeridis Ius Pontificium Cura et Impensis, Romae, 1925.

Wernz, F., et Vidal, P., *Ius Canonicum,* Vol. II: *De Personis,* Romae: Apud Aedes Universitatis Gregorianae, 1923.

Wilkins, David, *Concilia Magnae Britanniae et Hiberniae,* 4 vols., London, 1737.

Periodicals

Bogoslovni Vestnik, Ljubljana, Jugo-Slavia, 1921 — .

Catholic Historical Review, Washington, 1920 — .

Articles

Rozman, Gregor, "Cerkveno arhivno pravo" — *Bogoslovni Vestnik,* Leto IV, 1924, 145-155.

Stratemeir, G., "The Vatican School of Palaeography, Diplomatics and Archivistics" — *Catholic Historical Review,* XV (N. S. IX, 1929), 63-71.

BIOGRAPHICAL NOTE

William Francis Louis was born on August 25, 1904, at Jersey City, New Jersey. He received his primary education at St. Bridget's Parochial School and four years later was graduated from St. Peter's Preparatory School in the same city. He later attended Seton Hall College, South Orange, New Jersey, where he received the degrees of Bachelor of Arts in 1930 and Master of Arts in 1932. Upon the completion of his studies at the Immaculate Conception Seminary, Darlington, New Jersey, which was then affiliated with Seton Hall College, he was ordained to the priesthood on May 26, 1934, by His Excellency, the Most Rev. Thomas J. Walsh, J.C.D., then Bishop, now Archbishop, of Newark. In September, 1938, he enrolled in the School of Canon Law at the Catholic University of America, from which institution he obtained the Baccalaureate in Canon Law in June, 1939, and the Licentiate in Canon Law in June, 1940.

ALPHABETICAL INDEX

CANON LAW STUDIES

1. Freriks, Rev. Celestine A., C.PP.S., J.C.D., Religious Congregations in Their External Relations, 121 pp., 1916.
2. Galliher, Rev. Daniel M., O.P., J.C.D., Canonical Elections, 117 pp., 1917.
3. Borkowski, Rev. Aurelius L., O.F.M., J.C.D., De Confraternitatibus Ecclesiasticis, 136 pp., 1918.
4. Castillo, Rev. Cayo, J.C.D., Disertación Historico-Canonica sobre la Potestad del Cabildo en Sede Vacante o Impedida del Vicario Capitular, 99 pp., 1919 (1918).
5. Kubelbeck, Rev. William J., S.T.B., J.C.D., The Sacred Penitentiaria and Its Relations to Faculties of Ordinaries and Priests, 129 pp., 1918.
6. Petrovits, Rev. Joseph, J.C., S.T.D., J.C.D., The New Church Law On Matrimony, X-461 pp., 1919.
7. Hickey, Rev. John J., S.T.B., J.C.D., Irregularities and Simple Impediments in the New Code of Canon Law, 100 pp., 1920.
8. Klekotka, Rev. Peter J., S.T.B., J.C.D., Diocesan Consultors, 179 pp., 1920.
9. Wanenmacher, Rev. Francis, J.C.D., The Evidence in Ecclesiastical Procedure Affecting the Marriage Bond, 1920 (Printed 1935).
10. Golden, Rev. Henry Francis, J.C.D., Parochial Benefices in the New Code, IV-119 pp., 1921 (Printed 1925).
11. Koudelka, Rev. Charles J., J.C.D., Pastors, Their Rights and Duties According to the New Code of Canon Law, 211 pp., 1921.
12. Melo, Rev. Antonius, O.F.M., J.C.D., De Exemptione Regularium, X-188 pp., 1921.
13. Schaaf, Rev. Valentine Theodore, O.F.M., S.T.B., J.C.D., The Cloister, X-180 pp., 1921.
14. Burke, Rev. Thomas Joseph, S.T.D., J.C.D., Competence in Ecclesiastical Tribunals, IV-117 pp., 1922.
15. Leech, Rev. George Leo, J.C.D., A Comparative Study of the Constitution, "Apostolicae Sedis" and the "Codex Juris Canonici," 179 pp., 1922.
16. Motry, Rev. Hubert Louis, S.T.D., J.C.D., Diocesan Faculties According to the Code of Canon Law, II-167 pp., 1922.
17. Murphy, Rev. George Lawrence, J.C.D., Delinquencies and Penalties in the Administration and Reception of the Sacraments, IV-121 pp., 1923.
18. O'Reilly, Rev. John Anthony, S.T.B., J.C.D., Ecclesiastical Sepulture in the New Code of Canon Law, II-129 pp., 1923.
19. Michalicka, Rev. Wenceslas Cyrill, O.S.B., J.C.D., Judicial Procedure in Dismissal of Clerical Exempt Religious, 107 pp., 1923.
20. Dargin, Rev. Edward Vincent, S.T.B., J.C.D., Reserved Cases According to the Code of Canon Law, IV-103, pp. 1924.
21. Godfrey, Rev. John A., S.T.B., J.C.D., The Right of Patronage According to the Code of Canon Law, 153 pp., 1924.
22. Hagedorn, Rev. Francis Edward, J.C.D., General Legislation on Indulgences, II-154 pp., 1924.

23. King, Rev. James Ignatius, J.C.D., The Administration of the Sacraments to Dying Non-Catholics, V-141 pp., 1924.
24. Winslow, Rev. Francis Joseph, O.F.M., J.C.D., Vicars and Prefects Apostolic, IV-149 pp., 1924.
25. Correa, Rev. Jose Servelion, S.T.L., J.C.D., La Potestad Legislativa de la Iglesia Catolica, IV-127 pp., 1925.
26. Dugan, Rev. Henry Francis, A.M., J.C.D., The Judiciary Department of the Diocesan Curia, 87 pp., 1925.
27. Keller, Rev. Charles Frederick, S.T.B., J.C.D., Mass Stipends, 167 pp., 1925.
28. Paschang, Rev. John Linus, J.C.D., The Sacramentals According to the Code of Canon Law, 129 pp., 1925.
29. Pointek, Rev. Cyrillus, O.F.M., S.T.B., J.C.D., De Indulto Exclaustrationis necnon Saecularizationis, XIII-289 pp., 1925.
30. Kearney, Rev. Richard Joseph, S.T.B., J.C.D., Sponsors at Baptism According to the Code of Canon Law, IV-127 pp., 1925.
31. Bartlett, Rev. Chester Joseph, A.M., LL.B., J.C.D., The Tenure of Parochial Property in the United States of America, V-108 pp., 1926.
32. Kilker, Rev. Adrian Jerome, J.C.D., Extreme Unction, V-425 pp., 1926.
33. McCormick, Rev. Robert Emmett, J.C.D., Confessors of Religious, VIII-266 pp., 1926.
34. Miller, Rev. Newton Thomas, J.C.D., Founded Masses According to the Code of Canon Law, VII-93 pp., 1926.
35. Roelker, Rev. Edward G., S.T.D., J.C.D., Principles of Privilege According to the Code of Canon Law, XI-166 pp., 1926.
36. Bakalarczyk, Rev. Richardus, M.I.C., J.U.D., De Novitiatu, VIII-208 pp., 1927.
37. Pizzuti, Rev. Lawrence, O.F.M., J.U.L., De Parochis Religiosis, 1927 (Not printed).
38. Bliley, Rev. Nicholas Martin, O.S.B., J.C.D., Altars According to the Code of Canon Law, XIX-132 pp., 1927.
39. Brown, Mr. Brendan Francis, A.B., LL.M., J.U.D., The Canonical Juristic Personality with Special Reference to Its Status in the United States of America, V-212 pp., 1927.
40. Cavanaugh, Rev. William Thomas, C.P., J.U.D., The Reservation of the Blessed Sacrament, VIII-101 pp., 1927.
41. Doheny, Rev. William J., C.S.C., A.B., J.U.D., Church Property: Modes of Acquisition, X-118 pp., 1927.
42. Feldhaus, Rev. Aloysius H., C.PP.S., J.C.D., Oratories, IX-141 pp., 1927.
43. Kelly, Rev. James Patrick, A.B., J.C.D., The Jurisdiction of the Simple Confessor, X-208 pp., 1927.
44. Neuberger, Rev. Nicholas J., J.C.D., Canon 6 or the Relation of the Codex Juris Canonici to the Preceding Legislation, V-95 pp., 1927.
45. O'Keefe, Rev. Gerald Michael, J.C.D., Matrimonial Dispensations, Powers of Bishops, Priests and Confessors, VIII-232 pp., 1927.

46. Quigley, Rev. Joseph, A.M., A.B., J.C.B., Condemned Societies, 139 pp., 1927.
47. Zaplotnik, Rev. Johannes Leo, J.C.D., De Vicariis Foraneis, X-142 pp., 1927.
48. Duskie, Rev. John Aloysius, A.B., J.C.D., The Canonical Status of the Orientals in the United States, VIII, 196 pp., 1928.
49. Hyland, Rev. Francis Edward, J.C.D., Excommunication, Its Nature, Historical Development and Effects, VIII-181 pp., 1928.
50. Reinmann, Rev. Gerald Joseph, O.M.C., J.C.D., The Third Order Secular of Saint Francis, 201 pp., 1928.
51. Schenk, Rev. Francis J., J.C.D., The Matrimonial Impediments of Mixed Religion and Disparity of Cult, XVI-318 pp., 1929.
52. Coady, Rev. John Joseph, S.T.D., J.U.D., A.M., The Appointment of Pastors, VIII-150 pp., 1929.
53. Kay, Thomas Henry, J.C.D., Competence in Matrimonial Procedure, VIII-164 pp., 1929.
54. Turner, Rev. Sidney Joseph, C.P., J.U.D., The Vow of Poverty, XLIX-217 pp., 1929.
55. Kearney, Rev. Raymond A., A.B., S.T.D., J.C.D., The Principles of Delegation, VII-149 pp., 1929.
56. Conran, Rev. Edward James, A.B., J.C.D., The Interdict, V-163 pp., 1930.
57. O'Neil, Rev. William H., J.C.D., Papal Rescripts of Favor, VII-218 pp., 1930.
58. Bastnagel, Rev. Clement Vincent, J.U.D., The Appointment of Parochial Adjutants and Assistants, XV-257 pp., 1930.
59. Ferry, Rev. William A., A.B., J.C.D., Stole Fees, V-135 pp., 1930.
60. Costello, Rev. John Michael, A.B., J.C.D., Domicile and Quasi-domicile, VII-201 pp., 1930.
61. Kremer, Rev. Michael Nicholas, A.B., S.T.B., J.C.D., Church Support in the United States, VI-1930.
62. Angulo, Rev. Luis, C.M., J.C.D., Legislación de la Iglesia sobre la intención en la Aplicación de la Santa Misa, VII-104 pp., 1931.
63. Frey, Rev. Wolfgang Norbert, O.S.B., A.B., J.C.D., The Act of Religious Profession, VIII-174 pp., 1931.
64. Roberts, Rev. James Brendan, A.B., J.C.D., The Banns of Marriage, XIV-140 pp., 1931.
65. Ryder, Rev. Raymond Aloysius, A.B., J.C.D., Simony, IX-151 pp., 1931.
66. Campagna, Rev. Angelo, Ph.D. J.U.D., Il Vicario Generale del Vescovo, VII-205 pp., 1931.
67. Cox, Rev. Joseph Godfrey, A.B., J.C.D., The Administration of Seminaries, VI-124 pp., 1931.
68. Gregory, Rev. Donald J., J.U.D., The Pauline Privilege, XV-165 p., 1931.
69. Donohue, Rev. John F., J.C.D., The Impediment of Crime-110 pp., 1931.

70. Dooley, Rev. Eugene A., O.M.I., J.C.D., Church Law On Sacred Relics, IX-143 pp., 1931.
71. Orth, Rev. Raymond Clement, O.M.C., J.C.D., The Approbation of Religious Institutes, 171 pp., 1931.
72. Pernicone, Rev. Joseph M., A.B., J.C.D., The Ecclesiastical Prohibition of Books, XII-267 pp., 1932.
73. Clinton, Rev. Connell, A.B., J.C.D., The Paschal Precept, IX-108 pp., 1932.
74. Donnelly, Rev. Francis B., A.M., S.T.L., J.C.D., The Diocesan Synod, VIII-125 pp., 1932.
75. Torrente, Rev. Camilo, C.M.F., J.C.D., Las Processiones Sagradas, V-145 pp., 1932.
76. Murphy, Rev. Edwin J., C.PP.S., J.C.D., Suspension Ex Informata Conscientia, XI-122 pp., 1932.
77. Mackenzie, Rev. Eric F., A.M., S.T.L., J.C.D., The Delict of Heresy in its Commission, Penalization, Absolution, VII-124 pp., 1932.
78. Lyons, Rev. Avitus E., S.T.B., J.C.D., The Collegiate Tribunal of First Instance, XI-147 pp., 1932.
79. Connolly, Rev. Thomas A., J.C.D., Appeals, XI-195 pp., 1932.
80. Sangmeister, Rev. Joseph V., A.B., J.C.D., Force and Fear as Precluding Matrimonial Consent, V-211 pp., 1932.
81. Jaeger, Rev. Leo A., A.B., J.C.D., The Administration of Vacant and Quasi-vacant Episcopal Sees in the United States, IX-229 pp., 1932.
82. Rimlinger, Rev. Herbert T., J.C.D., Error Invalidating Matrimonial Consent, VII-79 pp., 1932.
83. Barrett, Rev. John D. M., S.S., J.C.D., A Comparative Study of the Third Plenary Council of Baltimore and the Code, IX-221 pp., 1932.
84. Carberry, Rev. John J., Ph.D., S.T.D., J.C.D., The Juridical Form of Marriage, X-177 pp., 1934.
85. Dolan, Rev. John L., A.B., J.C.D., The Defensor Vinculi, XII-157 pp., 1934.
86. Hannan, Rev. Jerome D., A.M., S.T.D., LL.B., J.C.D., The Canon Law of Wills, IX-517 pp., 1934.
87. Lemieux, Rev. Delisle A., A.M., J.C.D., The Sentence in Ecclesiastical Procedure, IX-131 pp., 1934.
88. O'Rourke, Rev. James J., A.B., J.C.D., Parish Registers, VII-109 pp., 1934.
89. Timlin, Rev. Bartholomew, O.F.M., A.M., J.C.D., Conditional Matrimonial Consent, X-381 pp., 1934.
90. Wahl, Rev. Francis X., A.B., J.C.D., The Matrimonial Impediments of Consanguinity and Affinity, VI-125 pp., 1934.
91. White, Rev. Robert J., A.B., LL.B., S.T.B., J.C.D., Canonical Ante-Nuptial Promises and the Civil Law, VI-152 pp., 1934.
92. Herrera, Rev. Antonio Parra, O.C.D., J.C.D., Legislación Eclesiástica sobre el Ayuno y la Abstinencia, XI-191 pp., 1935.

93. Kennedy, Rev. Edwin J., J.C.D., The Special Matrimonial Process in Cases of Evident Nullity, X-165 pp., 1935.
94. Manning, Rev. John J., A.B., J.C.D., Presumption of Law in Matrimonial Procedure, XI-111 pp., 1935.
95. Moeder, Rev. John M., J.C.D., The Proper Bishop for Ordination and Dimissorial Letters, VII-135 pp., 1935.
96. O'Mara, Rev. William A., A.B., J.C.D., Canonical Causes For Matrimonial Dispensations, IX-155 pp., 1935.
97. Reilly, Rev. Peter, J.C.D., Residence of Pastors, IX-81 pp., 1935.
98. Smith, Rev. Mariner T., O.P., S.T.L., J.C.D., The Penal Law For Religious, VII-169 pp., 1935.
99. Whalen, Rev. Donald W., A.M., J.C.D., The Value of Testimonial Evidence in Matrimonial Procedure, XIII-297 pp., 1935.
100. Cleary, Rev. Joseph F., J.C.D., Canonical Limitations on the Alienation of Church Property, VIII-141 pp., 1936.
101. Glynn, Rev. John C., J.C.D., The Promoter of Justice, XX-337 pp., 1936.
102. Brennan, Rev. James H., S.S., A.M., S.T.B., J.C.D., The Simple Convalidation of Marriage, VI-135 pp., 1937.
103. Brunini, Rev. Joseph Bernard, J.C.D., The Clerical Obligations of Canons 139 and 142, X-121 pp., 1937.
104. Connor, Rev. Maurice, A.B., J.C.D., The Administrative Removal of Pastors, VIII-159 pp., 1937.
105. Guilfoyle, Rev. Merlin Joseph, J.C.D., Custom, XI-144 pp., 1937.
106. Hughes, Rev. James Austin, A.B., A.M., J.C.D., Witnesses in Criminal Trials of Clerics, IX-140 pp., 1937.
107. Jansen, Rev. Raymond J., A.B., S.T.L., J.C.D., Canonical Provisions for Catechetical Instruction, VII-153 pp., 1937.
108. Kealy, Rev. John James, A.B., J.C.D., The Introductory Libellus in Church Court Procedure, XI-121 pp., 1937.
109. McManus, Rev. James Edward, C.SS.R., J.C.D., The Administration of Temporal Goods in Religious Institutes, XVI-196 pp., 1937.
110. Moriarity, Rev. Eugene James, J.C.D., Oaths in Ecclesiastical Courts, X-115 pp., 1937.
111. Rainer, Rev. Eligius George, C.SS.R., J.C.D., Suspension of Clerics, XVII-249 pp., 1937.
112. Reilly, Rev. Thomas F., C.SS.R., J.C.D., Visitation of Religious, VI-195 pp., 1938.
113. Moriarty, Rev. Francis E., C.SS.R., J.C.D., The Extraordinary Absolution from Censures, XV-334 pp., 1938.
114. Connolly, Rev. Nicholas P., J.C.D., The Canonical Erection of Parishes, X-132 pp., 1938.
115. Donovan, Rev. James Joseph, J.C.D., The Pastor's Obligation in Prenuptial Investigation, XII-322 pp., 1938.
116. Harrigan, Rev. Robert J., M.A., S.T.B., J.C.D., The Radical Sanation of Invalid Marriages, VIII-208 pp., 1938.

117. Boffa, Rev. Conrad Humbert, J.C.D., Canonical Provisions for Catholic Schools, X-211 pp., 1939.
118. Parsons, Rev. Anscar John, O.F.M. Cap., J.C.D., Canonical Elections, XII-236 pp., 1939.
119. Reilly, Rev. Edward Michael, A.B., J.C.D., The General Norms of Dispensation, X-156 pp., 1939.
120. Ryan, Rev. Gerald Aloysius, A.B., J.C.D., Principles of Episcopal Jurisdiction, XII-172 pp., 1939.
121. Burton, Rev. Francis James, C.S.C., A.B., J.C.D., A Commentary on Canon 1125, X-222 pp., 1940.
122. Miaskiewicz, Rev. Francis Sigismund, J.C.D., Supplied Jurisdiction According to Canon 209, XII-340 pp., 1940.
123. Rice, Rev. Patrick William, A.B., J.C.D., Proof of Death in Prenuptial Investigation, VIII-156 pp., 1940.
124. Anglin, Rev. Thomas Francis, M.S., J.C.L., The Eucharistic Fast.
125. Coleman, Rev. John Jerome, J.C.L., The Minister of Confirmation.
126. Downs, Rev. John Emmanuel, A.B., J.C.L., The Concept of Clerical Immunity.
127. Esswein, Rev. Anthony Albert, J.C.L., Extrajudicial Penal Powers of Ecclesiastical Superiors.
128. Farrell, Rev. Benjamin Francis, M.A., S.T.L., J.C.L., The Rights and Duties of the Local Ordinary Regarding Congregations of Women Religious of Pontifical Approval.
129. Feeney, Rev. Thomas John, A.B., S.T.L., J.C.L., Restitutio in Integrum.
130. Findlay, Rev. Stephen William, O.S.B., A.B., J.C.L., Canonical Norms Governing the Deposition and Degradation of Clerics.
131. Goodwine, Rev. John, A.B., S.T.L., J.C.L., The Right of the Church to Acquire Property.
132. Heston, Rev. Edward Louis, C.S.C., Ph.D., S.T.D., J.C.L., The Alienation of Church Property in the United States.
133. Hogan, Rev. James John, A.B., S.T.L., J.C.L., Judicial Advocates and Procurators.
134. Kealy, Rev. Thomas M., A.B., Litt. B., J.C.L., Dowry of Women Religious.
135. Keene, Rev. Michael James, O.S.B., J.C.L., Religious Ordinaries and Canon 198.
136. Kerin, Rev. Charles A., S.S., M.A., S.T.B., J.C.L., The Privation of Christian Burial.
137. Louis, Rev. William Francis, M.A., J.C.L., Diocesan Archives.
138. McDevitt, Rev. Gilbert Joseph, A.B., J.C.L., Legitimacy and Legitimation.
139. McDonough, Rev. Thomas Joseph, A.B., J.C.L., Apostolic Administrators.
140. Meier, Rev. Carl Anthony, A.B., J.C.L., Penal Administrative Procedure Against Negligent Pastors.
141. Schmidt, Rev. John Rogg, A.B., J.C.L., The Principles of Authentic Interpretation in Canon 17 of the Code of Canon Law.

142. Slafkosky, Rev. Andrew Leonard, A.B., J.C.L., The Canonical Episcopal Visitation of the Diocese.
143. Swoboda, Rev. Innocent Robert, O.F.M., J.C.L., Ignorance in Relation to the Imputability of Delicts.
144. Dubé, Rev. Arthur Joseph, A.B., J.C.L., The General Principles for the Reckoning of Time in Canon Law.
145. McBride, Rev. James T., A.B., J.C.L., Incardination and Excardination of Seculars.

www.ingramcontent.com/pod-product-compliance
Lightning Source LLC
LaVergne TN
LVHW050159080826
844660LV00012B/318
9780813223261